LangFlow for Developers

A Hands-On Guide to Building Powerful AI Agents and Workflows

©

Written By

Camila Jones

Copyright Page

LangFlow for Developers: A Hands-On Guide to Building Powerful AI Agents and Workflows
© 2025 Camila Jones

Disclaimer:
The author and publisher have made every effort to ensure the accuracy and completeness of the information in this book. However, the author and publisher make no warranties of any kind, either express or implied, regarding the accuracy, completeness, or adequacy of the information in this book. The content is provided "as is" and the reader assumes all responsibility for the use of the information provided.

Trademark Notice:
All brand names and product names mentioned in this book are trademarks or registered trademarks of their respective companies.

Table of Content

Preface

About This Book

Welcome to **"LangFlow for Developers: A Hands-On Guide to Building Powerful AI Agents and Workflows."** This book is designed to be your comprehensive companion in mastering LangFlow, a cutting-edge framework for developing intelligent AI agents and orchestrating complex workflows. Whether you are a seasoned developer looking to enhance your AI capabilities or a newcomer eager to dive into the world of AI-driven automation, this guide offers the knowledge and practical skills you need to succeed.

LangFlow stands at the intersection of artificial intelligence and workflow automation, providing developers with the tools to create sophisticated AI agents that can perform a variety of tasks, from simple data processing to complex decision-making processes. This book demystifies LangFlow, breaking down its components, features, and best practices into manageable, easy-to-understand sections.

Throughout this book, you will find a blend of theoretical insights and practical applications. Each chapter is meticulously crafted to guide you through the process of building, deploying, and optimizing AI agents using LangFlow. With step-by-step tutorials, real-world examples, and hands-on projects, you will gain the confidence and competence to leverage LangFlow effectively in your development projects.

Who Should Read This Book

"LangFlow for Developers" is tailored for a diverse audience of developers and technologists who are interested in harnessing the power of AI within their workflows. Whether you are:

- **Beginner Developers:** If you are new to AI and workflow automation, this book provides a solid foundation, introducing you to essential concepts and guiding you through your first LangFlow projects.

- **Experienced Developers:** For those with a background in software development and a basic understanding of AI, this guide delves deeper into advanced LangFlow features, optimization techniques, and integration strategies to enhance your existing skill set.
- **Data Scientists and AI Enthusiasts:** If your focus is on data analysis, machine learning, or AI model deployment, this book demonstrates how LangFlow can streamline your processes and amplify your AI projects.
- **Technical Managers and Team Leads:** For professionals overseeing development teams or AI projects, this book offers insights into implementing LangFlow within your organization, promoting efficient workflows, and fostering innovation.

How to Use This Book

To get the most out of **"LangFlow for Developers,"** it's recommended to follow the book in a sequential manner. Each chapter builds upon the previous ones, gradually increasing in complexity and depth. Here's how to navigate and utilize the content effectively:

1. **Start from the Beginning:** Begin with the **Introduction to LangFlow** to understand the basics, including what LangFlow is, its history, key features, and its role in the AI ecosystem.
2. **Set Up Your Environment:** Proceed to **Setting Up Your Development Environment** to install LangFlow, configure your tools, and ensure everything is ready for development.
3. **Master the Core Concepts:** Dive into the **Core Concepts of LangFlow** to grasp the fundamental components, such as AI agents, workflows, nodes, and data management.
4. **Hands-On Projects:** As you progress, engage with the **Hands-On Projects and Exercises** in each chapter. These practical assignments reinforce your learning and provide real-world experience in building and deploying AI agents.
5. **Explore Advanced Topics:** Once comfortable with the basics, move on to **Advanced AI Agent Development** and

other specialized chapters to enhance your skills and tackle more complex challenges.

6. **Utilize Supplementary Resources:** Make use of the **Appendix and Resources** section for additional materials, including sample code repositories, video tutorials, and community support channels.

7. **Apply Best Practices:** Pay close attention to the **Best Practices and Design Patterns** chapters to adopt industry-standard methodologies that ensure your projects are efficient, scalable, and maintainable.

8. **Stay Updated:** The **Future Trends and Innovations in LangFlow** chapter keeps you informed about the latest advancements and how to future-proof your LangFlow projects.

Interactive Elements:

Code Examples: Throughout the book, you will find complete and well-explained code snippets. These examples are designed to be copied, modified, and executed in your development environment, facilitating hands-on learning.

python

```python
# Example: Creating a simple AI agent in LangFlow

from langflow import LangFlowAgent

# Initialize the agent
agent = LangFlowAgent(name="SimpleAgent")

# Define a basic workflow
@agent.workflow
def greet_user(name: str) -> str:
    return f"Hello, {name}! Welcome to LangFlow."
```

```
# Execute the workflow
if __name__ == "__main__":
    response = agent.greet_user("Developer")
    print(response)
```

- *Explanation:* This code snippet demonstrates how to create a basic AI agent named "SimpleAgent" using LangFlow. The agent defines a workflow greet_user that takes a user's name as input and returns a personalized greeting. Running this script will output the greeting message.
- **Tables and Diagrams:** Visual aids such as tables, flowcharts, and diagrams are included to illustrate complex concepts and workflow architectures, enhancing your understanding.

LangFlow Component	Description
AI Agent	An autonomous entity that performs tasks using AI capabilities.
Workflow	A sequence of steps or processes that define how tasks are executed.
Node	A building block within a workflow that represents a specific action or operation.
Integration	Connecting LangFlow with external APIs, services, or databases to extend functionality.

-
    Explanation: This table provides a quick reference to key LangFlow components, offering clear definitions to aid in your learning journey.

Acknowledgments

Creating a comprehensive guide like **"LangFlow for Developers"** is a collaborative effort, and I am deeply grateful to everyone who contributed to its development:

- **The LangFlow Community:** Your active participation in forums, contributions to open-source projects, and willingness to share knowledge have been invaluable. Your feedback and real-world experiences have shaped the content of this book.
- **Beta Readers:** A special thank you to the developers and AI enthusiasts who reviewed early drafts of this book. Your insightful feedback, constructive criticism, and suggestions have greatly enhanced the quality and clarity of the content.
- **Technical Experts and Contributors:** I extend my gratitude to the experts in AI, machine learning, and workflow automation who provided their expertise and assisted in verifying the technical accuracy of the material.
- **Editorial and Design Teams:** Thank you to the editors and designers who meticulously reviewed the manuscript, ensuring that the content is not only accurate but also engaging and visually appealing.
- **Family and Friends:** Your unwavering support and encouragement have been a constant source of motivation throughout this project. Thank you for believing in me and providing the strength to see this book to fruition.
- **All Developers and Innovators:** To every developer pushing the boundaries of what's possible with AI and automation, this book is for you. Your dedication and creativity inspire me every day.

This book is a testament to the power of collaboration and the collective pursuit of knowledge. I hope that **"LangFlow for Developers: A Hands-On Guide to Building Powerful AI Agents and Workflows"** serves as a valuable resource in your development journey, empowering you to create innovative AI solutions that make a meaningful impact.

Thank you for choosing this book as your guide. Let's embark on this exciting journey together and unlock the full potential of LangFlow!

Chapter 1: Introduction to LangFlow

1.1. What is LangFlow?

LangFlow is a powerful framework designed for building and managing intelligent workflows and AI agents. It allows developers to integrate various AI capabilities, automate tasks, and streamline processes by building modular workflows that can interact with external APIs, services, and databases. At its core, LangFlow enables developers to design scalable, reusable, and efficient AI-driven applications through a visual interface and scripting environment.

LangFlow abstracts the complexity of creating AI agents by offering an intuitive, modular framework. It helps developers orchestrate AI tasks in a way that's easy to set up, maintain, and scale. Whether you're building a simple automation bot or a complex multi-agent system, LangFlow offers the tools and flexibility to bring your ideas to life.

LangFlow is not just for beginners—it caters to both novice developers and seasoned professionals by providing an easy-to-use interface while also supporting more advanced features and customizations.

The core functionality of LangFlow revolves around its ability to create, manage, and scale AI agents and workflows. Key features include:

- **Modular Workflows:** Developers can design workflows as a series of steps (or nodes), each performing a specific task like data processing, API calls, or model inference.
- **AI Agent Integration:** LangFlow supports AI agents that are capable of performing tasks autonomously. These agents can be configured to interact with other systems, make decisions, and carry out operations based on user input or external data.
- **Seamless API Integration:** LangFlow allows easy integration with third-party APIs and services. This makes it

ideal for scenarios where AI agents need to interact with databases, cloud services, or other external tools.

- **Real-Time Processing:** LangFlow supports both batch and real-time processing, enabling developers to choose the right approach based on the use case.
- **Extensibility:** LangFlow is designed to be extensible. You can add custom nodes, integrate new AI models, and extend its core functionality to suit your specific needs.

Here's an example of how you might create a simple AI agent in LangFlow:

python

```python
from langflow import LangFlowAgent

# Define the AI agent
agent = LangFlowAgent(name="GreetingAgent")

# Define a simple workflow
@agent.workflow
def greet_user(name: str) -> str:
    return f"Hello, {name}! How can I assist you today?"

# Execute the agent
if __name__ == "__main__":
    response = agent.greet_user("Developer")
    print(response)
```

Explanation: This code snippet creates an AI agent called GreetingAgent, defines a workflow greet_user, and then executes the workflow by calling the agent with a user name. The output would be a personalized greeting message.

1.2. History and Evolution of LangFlow

LangFlow was conceived as a solution to the complexity of managing AI systems and automating workflows within software applications. It started as an open-source project designed by a small team of AI developers who sought to provide a simpler, modular framework for building intelligent systems.

The initial version of LangFlow was built around the idea of combining AI capabilities with workflow automation tools, allowing developers to design applications without needing to handle the intricacies of underlying machine learning models or complex integration tasks.

Since its inception, LangFlow has evolved through several key stages:

- **Early Prototype (2018-2019):** The initial prototype of LangFlow was designed as a basic tool for automating simple AI-driven tasks.
- **Early Beta (2020):** As feedback from early users came in, LangFlow incorporated features like better API support, more flexible workflows, and a basic GUI for visual workflow management.
- **Major Release (2021):** LangFlow became a more mature framework, introducing advanced features like custom nodes, real-time data processing, and the ability to work with cloud services.
- **Current Version (2023):** LangFlow is now a fully-featured platform used by developers across a variety of industries, from AI research to business process automation.

Some of the major milestones in LangFlow's development include:

- **Version 1.0 (2020):** Introduction of the first stable release with basic AI agent functionality, modular workflows, and simplified API integration.
- **Version 2.0 (2021):** Major update with support for real-time processing, custom node development, and improved scalability.
- **Version 3.0 (2022):** Addition of a visual interface for building workflows, enhanced support for cloud and containerized deployments, and integration with popular AI frameworks like TensorFlow and PyTorch.
- **Version 4.0 (2023):** Current version, featuring expanded AI model support, advanced monitoring and logging features, and an even more user-friendly interface.

LangFlow's ongoing development continues to focus on enhancing its modularity, scalability, and integration capabilities to meet the growing demands of AI developers.

1.3. Key Features and Capabilities

LangFlow stands out in the AI ecosystem due to its unique combination of features:

- **Modularity:** LangFlow's modular approach allows developers to break down complex workflows into smaller, reusable components. This makes it easy to manage, extend, and scale projects over time.
- **Visual Workflow Designer:** The drag-and-drop visual interface allows developers to design workflows quickly and intuitively. You can visualize the data flow and see how components interact with each other.
- **AI Integration:** LangFlow offers seamless integration with AI models, enabling you to use pre-trained models or train your own models directly within the platform.
- **Real-Time Processing Support:** Unlike many workflow automation tools, LangFlow can handle real-time data streams,

making it suitable for time-sensitive applications such as customer support bots or data monitoring systems.

- **Extensibility:** LangFlow allows you to create custom nodes and workflows to meet your specific needs. This makes it highly adaptable to various industries, from healthcare to finance.

LangFlow's comparative advantages over other AI and workflow automation tools include:

- **Ease of Use:** Unlike other complex frameworks that require deep knowledge of AI or machine learning, LangFlow's modular design and visual interface lower the learning curve significantly.
- **Cross-Platform Compatibility:** LangFlow is compatible with multiple cloud platforms, databases, and external services, providing flexibility in deployment options.
- **Focus on Developer Experience:** While many AI tools are focused on research and experimentation, LangFlow is specifically built for developers looking to create production-ready AI agents and workflows quickly.

1.4. LangFlow in the AI Ecosystem

LangFlow occupies a unique position in the AI ecosystem by offering a framework that combines workflow automation with AI capabilities. While traditional machine learning tools like TensorFlow, PyTorch, and scikit-learn focus on building and training models, LangFlow allows developers to integrate these models into larger workflows that can automate tasks and make decisions autonomously.

LangFlow bridges the gap between AI model development and practical application by enabling easy orchestration of AI tasks and interaction with other systems. Its role in automating workflows and managing AI agents makes it an ideal tool for deploying AI-powered applications at scale.

LangFlow has numerous practical use cases across various industries. Some examples include:

- **Customer Support Automation:** Building AI-powered chatbots that handle customer queries and automate responses based on user input.
- **Data Processing Pipelines:** Designing workflows for processing large datasets, integrating AI models for analysis and decision-making.
- **Business Process Automation:** Streamlining repetitive business tasks such as report generation, inventory management, or data entry.
- **IoT Integrations:** Automating interactions between IoT devices and AI systems for real-time monitoring and data processing.

The flexibility of LangFlow makes it applicable to a wide range of industries, from healthcare to retail, enabling organizations to implement intelligent systems that optimize operations and improve user experiences.

1.5. Benefits of Using LangFlow for Developers

LangFlow is designed to improve developer productivity in several ways:

- **Simplified Workflow Design:** With the visual workflow designer, developers can build and iterate on complex workflows quickly without needing to write extensive code.
- **Pre-Built Components:** LangFlow provides a library of pre-built nodes and functions that handle common tasks like API calls, database queries, and data transformations, saving developers time.
- **Quick Deployment:** The platform's cloud integration and containerization capabilities enable rapid deployment and

scaling, reducing the time it takes to bring AI-driven applications to production.

LangFlow offers developers both flexibility and scalability in their projects:

- **Customizability:** Developers can easily extend LangFlow by creating custom nodes or integrating third-party services and APIs. This ensures that the platform can be adapted to meet specific needs.
- **Scalability:** LangFlow is designed to handle both small and large-scale applications. Whether you're building a simple automation bot or a complex multi-agent system, LangFlow's modular architecture makes it easy to scale as your needs grow.
- **Cloud and On-Premises Support:** LangFlow can be deployed on a variety of environments, including local servers, cloud platforms, and containerized solutions like Docker, providing the flexibility to choose the best option based on your infrastructure requirements.

In summary, **LangFlow** is a dynamic, versatile framework that provides developers with everything they need to create and manage intelligent workflows and AI agents. By combining ease of use with powerful functionality, it allows you to focus on building robust, scalable AI applications while abstracting much of the complexity involved in integrating AI models and automating processes. This chapter has given you an overview of LangFlow's capabilities, its positioning in the AI ecosystem, and the benefits it brings to developers. As we continue, you'll see how to practically apply LangFlow to real-world projects and enhance your development processes.

Chapter 2: Setting Up Your Development Environment

2.1. System Requirements

Before you can start building your LangFlow projects, it's essential to ensure your development environment meets the necessary system requirements. This section will guide you through the hardware and software specifications required to run LangFlow smoothly, as well as the recommended tools and plugins that will enhance your development experience.

Hardware Requirements: LangFlow is designed to run efficiently on a wide range of systems, but certain hardware specifications will ensure optimal performance, especially when working with complex AI models or large-scale workflows.

- **CPU:** A multi-core processor (Intel i5/Ryzen 5 or higher recommended). LangFlow benefits from parallel processing, and a multi-core CPU will speed up data processing and AI agent execution.
- **RAM:** At least 8 GB of RAM. If you're working on larger AI models or more extensive workflows, 16 GB or more is highly recommended.
- **Storage:** At least 10 GB of free disk space. LangFlow itself doesn't require a large amount of disk space, but additional storage will be needed for datasets, models, and logs.
- **Graphics:** A dedicated GPU is optional but beneficial if you plan on running deep learning models (e.g., TensorFlow or PyTorch). LangFlow can leverage GPU acceleration for these tasks.

Software Requirements: LangFlow is cross-platform and can be installed on Windows, macOS, and Linux. Below are the software specifications for each operating system.

- Operating System:

- Windows 10/11 (64-bit)
- macOS 10.15 (Catalina) or later
- Ubuntu 20.04 or later (for Linux users)
- **Python:** LangFlow requires Python 3.7 or later. It's essential to install Python on your system, as LangFlow is built on top of Python libraries.
- Package Manager:
  - **pip:** Python's package manager for installing libraries and dependencies.
  - **Docker (optional):** For containerized deployment or development, Docker is recommended for ensuring consistency across environments.
- **Dependencies:** LangFlow has several core dependencies that must be installed, including:
  - langflow (main LangFlow library)
  - numpy (for numerical operations)
  - requests (for HTTP requests)
  - flask or fastapi (for web interface support)

Here's a basic check for Python and pip version:

bash

```
python --version
pip --version
```

If these commands return the correct version, you're ready to proceed. If not, follow the installation guides for Python and pip for your operating system.

To make the development process smoother, the following tools and plugins are recommended:

- Integrated Development Environment (IDE):

- **VS Code**: A lightweight, versatile editor that supports Python development with extensions like Python, Pylance, and Jupyter Notebooks.
- **PyCharm**: A powerful IDE tailored for Python developers with features like intelligent code completion, debugging, and version control.
- Version Control:
  - **Git**: A distributed version control system essential for managing code versions and collaborating with others. Install Git to keep track of changes to your LangFlow projects.
- Docker (optional):
  - Docker can be used to containerize your LangFlow applications, ensuring they run consistently across different environments. It's particularly useful for deploying LangFlow-based systems in production.
- Virtual Environment:
  - **venv** or **virtualenv**: Creating a virtual environment helps isolate dependencies for LangFlow from the rest of your system, preventing potential conflicts.

2.2. Installing LangFlow

With the system requirements covered, we can now move on to the installation process. This section will guide you through setting up LangFlow from scratch.

Follow these steps to install LangFlow on your system:

Step 1: Install Python (if not already installed)

- Download Python 3.7 or later from the official Python website.
- Follow the installation instructions for your operating system. During installation, ensure that you select the option to add Python to your system's PATH.

Step 2: Install pip (if not already installed)

- pip is Python's package installer. It should be included with Python by default. You can check if pip is installed by running:

bash

```
pip --version
```

If it's not installed, you can follow the instructions on the official pip installation page.

Step 3: Install LangFlow

- Open a terminal or command prompt and execute the following command to install LangFlow:

bash

```
pip install langflow
```

This will download and install LangFlow along with its dependencies. Once installed, you can verify the installation by running:

bash

```
langflow --version
```

This should return the installed version of LangFlow.

Step 4: Optional - Install Docker (for containerization)

- If you plan to use Docker for your LangFlow applications, download and install Docker from here.

- After installation, you can verify Docker by running:

bash

```
docker --version
```

If you encounter issues during installation, here are some common solutions:

- Error: Permission Denied when installing packages:
  - This can happen if you're trying to install packages globally without the necessary permissions. To resolve this, use sudo (on Linux/macOS) or run the command prompt as Administrator (on Windows).

bash

```
sudo pip install langflow
```

- Error: Missing dependencies or version mismatches:
  - Make sure your Python and pip versions meet the required specifications. Update Python and pip by running:

bash

```
pip install --upgrade pip
```

- Error: Docker installation issues:
  - Ensure Docker is installed and running. If you're on Windows or macOS, you may need to enable Docker Desktop to run containerized applications.

2.3. Configuring Your Development Environment

After installation, it's essential to configure your development environment to work seamlessly with LangFlow. This section will guide you through the steps to set up your IDE, configure environment variables, and set up your system for optimal LangFlow development.

To begin developing with LangFlow, it's highly recommended to use an IDE or text editor that supports Python and provides features such as code completion, debugging, and syntax highlighting. Here's how to set up some popular editors:

- VS Code Setup:
  1. Install VS Code.
  2. Install the **Python extension** from the Extensions marketplace.
  3. Configure the **Python interpreter** by selecting it from the command palette (Ctrl+Shift+P → Python: Select Interpreter).
- PyCharm Setup:
  1. Install PyCharm.
  2. Set up a **Python virtual environment** in PyCharm for LangFlow projects.
  3. Configure Python paths in PyCharm's settings under **Project: Interpreter**.

Setting up environment variables is essential, especially when managing multiple projects or dependencies. Here's how you can configure Python and LangFlow for consistent development:

Python Environment: If you're using a virtual environment, activate it by running:
bash

```
source <your-venv>/bin/activate  # macOS/Linux
<your-venv>\Scripts\activate  # Windows
```

- **LangFlow Environment Variables:** If LangFlow requires specific environment variables (e.g., for API keys or paths), you can set them like so:

Linux/macOS:
bash

```
export LANGFLOW_API_KEY="your_api_key"
```

Windows:
bash

```
set LANGFLOW_API_KEY="your_api_key"
```

- Add these environment variables to your system's configuration file to make them persistent across sessions (e.g., .bashrc or .bash_profile on Linux/macOS).

2.4. Introduction to LangFlow CLI and GUI

LangFlow offers both a **Command-Line Interface (CLI)** and a **Graphical User Interface (GUI)** to help you interact with the platform. Here's an introduction to both.

CLI (Command-Line Interface): The LangFlow CLI allows you to execute commands and manage workflows directly from your terminal. The CLI is essential for tasks such as running workflows,

managing AI agents, and deploying applications.
Common CLI commands include:
bash

```
langflow init    # Initializes a new LangFlow project
langflow start   # Starts the LangFlow service
langflow run <file> # Runs a specific workflow file
```

- **GUI (Graphical User Interface):** LangFlow's GUI provides a more intuitive, drag-and-drop interface to design workflows and visualize data flows. The GUI makes it easier to connect nodes, set up integrations, and debug workflows without writing extensive code.
- **langflow start:** Starts the LangFlow service and initializes the necessary backend components for running AI agents and workflows.
- **langflow create <name>:** Creates a new LangFlow project or workflow.
- **langflow status:** Displays the current status of your LangFlow agent or workflow, including logs and error messages.
- **langflow help:** Lists all available commands and their descriptions.

2.5. Verifying the Installation

After installing and configuring LangFlow, it's important to verify that everything is working correctly.

Run the following command to verify that LangFlow is installed and functioning:

bash

This will run a basic test that ensures the installation is successful and that LangFlow can execute a simple workflow.

To ensure that LangFlow is fully operational, you should check the following:

- **Service Status:** Ensure the LangFlow service is running by using the langflow status command.
- **Test Workflow Execution:** Create a simple test workflow to confirm that LangFlow can process tasks correctly.
- **Logs:** Review system logs for any errors or warnings that might indicate problems.

By following these steps, you will have a fully functional LangFlow development environment and be ready to start building your AI-powered workflows and agents.

With this setup, you're now ready to begin developing with LangFlow, and you can confidently move on to creating your first projects. If you encounter any issues during setup, refer to the troubleshooting section, or consult the LangFlow community for further support.

Chapter 3: Core Concepts of LangFlow

3.1. Understanding AI Agents

An **AI agent** in LangFlow refers to an autonomous entity that can carry out tasks and make decisions based on its environment or data. AI agents are designed to perform specific functions within a system, often interacting with other agents or external services, and can be programmed to follow rules or learn from experience. These agents can be simple or complex, depending on the task they are designed to handle.

There are several types of AI agents, each serving a different purpose based on its intelligence level, autonomy, and the complexity of tasks it can perform:

- **Reactive Agents**: These agents respond to stimuli from their environment based on predefined rules. They do not have memory or the ability to learn from past experiences. For example, a simple AI agent that checks data against a set of conditions and performs a predefined action is a reactive agent.
- **Deliberative Agents**: Deliberative agents have a model of the world and use this model to plan and make decisions. These agents can make decisions based on past actions and future goals. They typically operate in more complex environments, where they need to consider multiple options before choosing the best course of action.
- **Learning Agents**: These agents can learn from their experiences. They typically use machine learning techniques to adjust their behavior based on feedback or data over time. An example of a learning agent might be a recommendation system that improves its recommendations as it gathers more data about users' preferences.
- **Autonomous Agents**: These agents have the highest level of independence, capable of making decisions, learning from their actions, and taking actions without requiring human

intervention. Autonomous agents are particularly useful in applications like robotics or autonomous vehicles.

AI agents are responsible for carrying out a wide range of tasks, depending on their design. Some key roles and responsibilities include:

- **Task Automation**: AI agents automate repetitive tasks. For example, a data processing agent can automatically clean and transform raw data into a structured format for analysis.
- **Decision-Making**: Deliberative and learning agents are responsible for making decisions based on the available data. This is particularly important in environments where dynamic decision-making is required, such as in business analytics or autonomous systems.
- **Interaction with Other Agents**: Many AI agents work in a multi-agent system where they collaborate with other agents. Each agent in this system might have a specialized role, such as handling data processing, managing requests, or communicating with external systems.
- **Data Collection and Processing**: AI agents often gather data from different sources, process it, and pass it on for further analysis or actions. For example, a web scraping agent collects data from websites and sends it to a data storage system.

Code Example: Creating an AI Agent in LangFlow

python

```python
from langflow import LangFlowAgent

# Define a simple reactive AI agent
agent = LangFlowAgent(name="DataCleanerAgent")

@agent.workflow
```

```python
def clean_data(input_data):
    # Remove null values and standardize column names
    cleaned_data = input_data.dropna()
    cleaned_data.columns = [col.lower().replace(" ", "_") for col in cleaned_data.columns]
    return cleaned_data


if __name__ == "__main__":
    input_data = load_data("raw_data.csv")  # Hypothetical data load function
    cleaned_data = agent.clean_data(input_data)
    print(cleaned_data)
```

Explanation: This code defines a simple **reactive agent** called DataCleanerAgent, which performs data cleaning on a provided dataset by removing null values and standardizing column names. The agent's workflow (clean_data) is triggered by input data, and the cleaned data is returned after processing.

3.2. Workflows Explained

A **workflow** in LangFlow is a series of interconnected steps (or nodes) that define how data is processed and how tasks are executed. Workflows can be designed visually or programmatically, depending on the complexity of the tasks and the preferences of the developer.

Workflows typically follow a linear or branching structure:

- **Linear Workflow**: Tasks are executed in sequence, one after the other.
- **Branching Workflow**: Tasks can branch into different paths based on conditions or outcomes from previous tasks.

In LangFlow, workflows can be as simple as a few nodes or as complex as a multi-step process involving multiple agents and external systems.

The main components of a LangFlow workflow include:

- **Nodes**: Represent individual tasks or actions, such as data processing, API calls, or decision-making processes.
- **Edges**: Define the flow of data between nodes, ensuring that the output of one task serves as the input to the next.
- **Workflows**: A collection of nodes and edges that together define the complete sequence of tasks.

Workflows are designed by linking these nodes, allowing data to flow from one task to the next. LangFlow provides an intuitive interface for building and managing these connections.

3.3. Nodes and Components in LangFlow

In LangFlow, **nodes** are the building blocks of workflows, each performing a specific task. There are several types of nodes, such as:

- **Input Nodes**: These nodes handle the data input into the system, such as reading from files or receiving user input.
- **Processing Nodes**: Nodes that perform operations on the data, such as cleaning, transforming, or analyzing it.
- **Output Nodes**: These nodes handle the final output, such as saving results to a database or sending an email notification.
- **Decision Nodes**: These nodes evaluate conditions and decide which path the workflow should take, enabling branching logic.
- **Integration Nodes**: Used to connect to external systems, APIs, or databases.

LangFlow allows you to **customize nodes** to extend their functionality. This can be done by creating your own custom nodes or by modifying existing nodes. Custom nodes might include specific data transformations, machine learning model calls, or third-party integrations that are unique to your application.

Here's how you might create a custom node:

python

```python
from langflow import Node

class CustomDataProcessor(Node):
    def process(self, input_data):
        # Custom data processing logic
        processed_data = input_data.apply(lambda x: x * 2)  # Example: multiplying each value by 2
        return processed_data

# Adding the custom node to a workflow
@agent.workflow
def process_data(input_data):
    custom_processor = CustomDataProcessor()
    return custom_processor.process(input_data)
```

Explanation: The CustomDataProcessor class extends LangFlow's Node class and defines its own process method to handle custom data transformations. This node can be used in workflows just like any other built-in node.

3.4. Data Flow and Management

Data flow refers to how data moves through the workflow, passing from one node to another. LangFlow uses several common data structures and formats to manage this flow:

- **Pandas DataFrame**: Commonly used for tabular data, where rows represent data entries and columns represent variables.
- **JSON**: Often used for exchanging data between systems or APIs, especially for hierarchical data.
- **CSV/Excel**: Used for storing and processing large datasets.
- **Plain Text**: Simple text data, useful for logs or basic messages.

Each node in LangFlow accepts and returns data in these formats, ensuring compatibility with other nodes and external systems.

LangFlow enables the creation of **data pipelines**, where data flows through various nodes to be transformed, analyzed, and output. These pipelines can be linear or branched and can involve operations such as:

- **Data Cleaning**: Removing missing values, handling duplicates, and standardizing data.
- **Data Transformation**: Changing data formats, aggregating values, or applying mathematical operations.
- **Data Output**: Writing the processed data to a file, database, or external service.

A simple data pipeline in LangFlow might look like this:

python

```python
from langflow import LangFlowAgent

# Define the agent and workflow
agent = LangFlowAgent(name="DataProcessingAgent")
```

```python
@agent.workflow
def process_pipeline(raw_data):
    cleaned_data = clean_data(raw_data)
    transformed_data = transform_data(cleaned_data)
    output_data(transformed_data)
    return transformed_data
```

Explanation: This pipeline takes raw_data, processes it through cleaning and transformation nodes, and outputs the result. The process is seamless, and the data flows from one step to the next.

3.5. Integration with External APIs and Services

LangFlow allows developers to integrate with external APIs and services, enabling the use of additional functionalities such as accessing third-party databases, sending HTTP requests, or calling external AI models.

Integration nodes are used to handle these connections. For example, you might use an integration node to fetch weather data from an API:

python

```python
import requests

def fetch_weather_data(city):
    url = f"https://api.weatherapi.com/v1/current.json?key=YOUR_API_KEY&q={city}"
    response = requests.get(url)
    return response.json()
```

Explanation: The fetch_weather_data function connects to an external weather API to retrieve data. This data can then be passed to other nodes in the LangFlow workflow for further processing.

When integrating APIs and external services, it's essential to follow best practices to ensure reliability, security, and performance:

- **Authentication**: Always use secure authentication methods like API keys, OAuth, or JWT tokens to protect your data.
- **Error Handling**: Properly handle errors by checking API responses and implementing retry mechanisms if the connection fails.
- **Rate Limiting**: Ensure that your API calls respect the service's rate limits to avoid service disruptions.
- **Data Validation**: Always validate the data returned from external services to ensure it meets the expected format and values before processing it in your workflow.

In this chapter, we've covered the core concepts of LangFlow, including the fundamental building blocks such as AI agents, workflows, nodes, and data flow. You've also learned about integrating external services and how to effectively manage data through LangFlow's modular architecture. With these concepts in mind, you're well-equipped to start building powerful, AI-driven workflows with LangFlow.

Chapter 4: Building Your First AI Agent

4.1. Planning Your AI Agent

Before you start developing an AI agent in LangFlow, it's essential to plan out the objectives and scope of the agent, as well as the specific requirements it needs to fulfill. Planning helps to ensure that your agent is functional, scalable, and well-organized. In this section, we'll guide you through defining the objectives of your AI agent and mapping out the functional requirements.

The first step in creating any AI agent is clearly defining its purpose and the tasks it will perform. This involves answering key questions such as:

- **What problem will this AI agent solve?**: Identify the primary task your agent will address, such as automating data entry, answering user queries, or processing information.
- **What are the inputs and outputs?**: Determine the type of data your agent will handle. For instance, will it be working with text, numbers, images, or a combination of these?
- **What level of complexity is required?**: Is the agent expected to perform a simple task like filtering data, or does it require advanced decision-making capabilities, such as using machine learning models or external APIs?

Let's take the example of an AI agent that provides basic customer support:

- **Objective**: The agent will automatically respond to frequently asked questions about a product's features, pricing, and shipping.
- **Scope**: The agent will answer specific customer queries, but will not handle complex interactions or complaints.

Defining these details early on will guide the development process and help you avoid unnecessary complexity or functionality that isn't needed.

Once you've defined the objectives and scope of the AI agent, the next step is to map out the functional requirements. These requirements outline the tasks and actions the agent must be able to perform. For example, for our customer support agent:

- **Task 1**: Receive customer queries via text.
- **Task 2**: Analyze the query and match it to predefined answers.
- **Task 3**: Provide a response from the available knowledge base.
- **Task 4**: If the query is unrecognized, redirect the user to a human agent.

This list of tasks helps ensure that the AI agent has the right capabilities and that each functionality is properly integrated into the workflow.

4.2. Creating a Basic AI Agent with LangFlow

With the planning stage complete, it's time to start building the AI agent. In LangFlow, creating an agent involves defining a series of workflows and linking them together in a logical sequence. Here's how to create your first basic AI agent.

We'll create a simple AI agent named **CustomerSupportAgent** that will respond to common customer queries. Below is a step-by-step guide to implement the agent.

Import LangFlow Library: First, we need to import LangFlow to start defining the agent and its workflows.
python

```python
from langflow import LangFlowAgent
```

Define the AI Agent: Create an instance of the agent using the LangFlowAgent class. We'll name it "CustomerSupportAgent."
python

```python
agent = LangFlowAgent(name="CustomerSupportAgent")
```

Define a Basic Workflow: We'll define a workflow for handling customer queries. The workflow will check if the query matches predefined FAQs and return a response.
python

```python
@agent.workflow
def handle_query(query: str) -> str:
    # Predefined responses
    faqs = {
        "price": "The price of the product is $49.99.",
        "shipping": "We offer free shipping worldwide.",
        "return policy": "You can return the product within 30 days of purchase."
    }

    # Check for matching query
    for keyword, response in faqs.items():
        if keyword in query.lower():
            return response
    return "Sorry, I couldn't find an answer to that question."
```

Run the Agent: Finally, we'll run the agent to see it in action. The agent will process a sample query and return a response.
python

```python
if __name__ == "__main__":
    user_query = "What is the price of the product?"
```

```python
response = agent.handle_query(user_query)
print(response)
```

Explanation: In this example, the CustomerSupportAgent is set up to check if a query matches any of the predefined FAQs. If a match is found, it returns the corresponding answer; otherwise, it returns a default message.

When creating your agent, there are a few configuration settings that you might need to adjust depending on your use case:

- **Input Validation**: Ensure that the agent properly handles various types of input (e.g., text, numeric values).
- **Logging**: Enable logging for monitoring agent performance and tracking interactions.
- **Timeout Settings**: For agents interacting with external APIs, setting appropriate timeouts ensures that long-running operations do not block the agent's workflow.

python

```python
agent.config.logging_enabled = True  # Enable logging for debugging purposes
```

4.3. Configuring Input and Output Parameters

Once your AI agent is set up, it's important to configure how data will flow in and out of the system. LangFlow makes it easy to define input parameters (e.g., user queries) and output parameters (e.g., the agent's responses).

When dealing with input and output data, you must define the data types and ensure that they are valid. LangFlow supports common data types such as strings, numbers, lists, and dictionaries.

- **String Data Type**: For handling text input and output, such as customer queries or responses.
- **Integer and Float Data Types**: For numerical inputs or calculations.
- **List Data Type**: Useful when working with multiple items, such as a list of products or user preferences.

Here's an example of how to validate the input data type for the handle_query function:

python

```python
@agent.workflow
def handle_query(query: str) -> str:
    if not isinstance(query, str):
        return "Invalid input. Please provide a text query."

    # Processing logic
    faqs = {"price": "The price is $49.99.", "shipping": "Free worldwide shipping."}
    return faqs.get(query.lower(), "I don't understand your question.")
```

Explanation: In this example, the agent checks if the query parameter is a string. If not, it returns an error message. This ensures that the agent only processes valid data and avoids errors during execution.

Parameter mapping refers to the process of linking input data to the correct workflow steps. LangFlow provides flexible parameter mapping mechanisms that allow you to pass data between nodes efficiently.

For example, you might map a user's input to a specific agent task:

python

```python
@agent.workflow
def process_customer_request(name: str, request: str):
    # Map input parameters
    customer_name = name
    customer_request = request

    response = handle_query(customer_request)  # Passing request to the query handler
    return f"Hello, {customer_name}. {response}"
```

In this case, the parameters name and request are mapped to variables, which are then passed to the appropriate workflow steps.

4.4. Testing and Debugging Your AI Agent

Once your AI agent is implemented, it's important to test it thoroughly and debug any issues. This section covers common issues and solutions, along with tips on using debugging tools effectively.

- Issue: Agent Not Responding to Queries
  - **Solution**: Ensure that the agent's workflow is defined correctly and that the input is properly passed to the function.
- Issue: Invalid Output Format
  - **Solution**: Check that the output from your agent matches the expected data type (e.g., string or

dictionary). Implement validation checks to ensure consistent output.
- Issue: Agent Crashes on Unknown Input
  - **Solution**: Add error handling for unknown or unsupported input. Use a default response for unrecognized queries.

LangFlow provides built-in debugging tools that allow you to step through the agent's execution and identify issues:

- **Print Statements**: Add print statements to monitor the flow of data and track intermediate steps.
- **Logging**: Enable logging to capture detailed information about the agent's actions. This is helpful for diagnosing issues in production environments.

python

```python
import logging

# Enable logging
logging.basicConfig(level=logging.DEBUG)

@agent.workflow
def handle_query(query: str) -> str:
    logging.debug(f"Received query: {query}")

    # Handle query
    faqs = {"price": "The price is $49.99."}
    response = faqs.get(query.lower(), "Unknown query")

    logging.debug(f"Returning response: {response}")
    return response
```

4.5. Deploying Your First AI Agent

With your AI agent built and tested, the final step is deploying it to a production environment. This section will walk you through the available deployment options and strategies for LangFlow agents.

- **Local Deployment**: For simple projects or testing, you can run your AI agent locally on your machine. This is the quickest deployment method and is useful during development.
- **Cloud Deployment**: LangFlow supports deployment to cloud platforms like AWS, Azure, and Google Cloud. For scalable, production-grade deployments, cloud solutions are ideal.
- **Containerized Deployment**: Using Docker, you can containerize your LangFlow applications, ensuring that they run consistently across different environments.

Here's how to deploy your agent using Docker:

Create a Dockerfile:
dockerfile

```
FROM python:3.8-slim
RUN pip install langflow
COPY . /app
WORKDIR /app
CMD ["python", "agent.py"]
```

Build the Docker Image:
bash

```
docker build -t langflow-agent .
```

Run the Container:
bash

```bash
docker run -p 5000:5000 langflow-agent
```

After deploying your AI agent, it's important to verify that everything is working as expected:

- **Check Logs**: Review the application logs to ensure no errors occurred during deployment.
- **Test the Agent**: Interact with the deployed agent (either via CLI, GUI, or API) to confirm that it performs as expected.
- **Monitor Performance**: Use monitoring tools to track the agent's performance in the production environment and ensure it handles requests efficiently.

This chapter has provided a step-by-step guide to building your first AI agent using LangFlow. By planning the agent, configuring inputs and outputs, testing and debugging, and deploying to your chosen environment, you are well-equipped to begin developing production-ready AI agents for real-world applications.

Chapter 5: Advanced AI Agent Development

5.1. Enhancing AI Agents with Machine Learning Models

To develop more intelligent and capable AI agents, integrating **machine learning (ML)** models is a powerful way to improve decision-making, predictions, and problem-solving. In LangFlow, you can seamlessly integrate ML models into your workflows, allowing your agents to perform tasks that involve learning from data, making predictions, and adapting to new information over time.

LangFlow supports integration with popular machine learning frameworks such as **TensorFlow**, **PyTorch**, **scikit-learn**, and others. These frameworks provide pre-built algorithms and tools to train, test, and deploy machine learning models within your workflows.

For example, if you are using **TensorFlow** for a predictive task, you can integrate the model into LangFlow like this:

python

```python
import tensorflow as tf
from langflow import LangFlowAgent

# Load pre-trained TensorFlow model
model =
tf.keras.models.load_model('path_to_your_model.h5')

# Define the agent
agent = LangFlowAgent(name="MLAgent")
```

```python
# Define a workflow that uses the model
@agent.workflow
def predict_outcome(input_data):
    # Preprocess input data (e.g., scaling, reshaping)
    input_data = preprocess_data(input_data)

    # Make prediction using the trained model
    prediction = model.predict(input_data)
    return prediction
```

Explanation: In this example, we load a pre-trained TensorFlow model and define a LangFlow workflow (predict_outcome) that uses this model to make predictions based on the input data. The preprocess_data() function can be a custom function that prepares the data before passing it to the model.

When integrating machine learning into your AI agent, you have two main options: **using pre-trained models** or **training new models**. If you need to train a new model, here's an overview of the steps:

1. **Prepare Data**: Collect and clean the data required for training your model. This may involve labeling data, feature extraction, or normalizing values.
2. **Select a Model**: Choose a machine learning algorithm that fits your task. For instance, you could use a classification model for categorizing input or a regression model for making numerical predictions.
3. **Train the Model**: Use the chosen framework to train the model. Here's an example of training a simple regression model using **scikit-learn**:

python

```python
from sklearn.model_selection import train_test_split
from sklearn.linear_model import LinearRegression
from sklearn.datasets import make_regression

# Generate sample data
X, y = make_regression(n_samples=100, n_features=1,
noise=0.1)

# Split the data into training and testing sets
X_train, X_test, y_train, y_test = train_test_split(X, y,
test_size=0.2, random_state=42)

# Create and train the model
model = LinearRegression()
model.fit(X_train, y_train)

# Evaluate the model
score = model.score(X_test, y_test)
print(f"Model accuracy: {score:.2f}")
```

Explanation: This example generates sample data using make_regression(), splits it into training and testing sets, and then trains a **Linear Regression** model using **scikit-learn**. The model is evaluated on the test set, and the accuracy is printed.

4. **Deploy the Model**: After training, the model can be saved and deployed to your LangFlow agent, as shown in the previous section. This allows your agent to make real-time predictions based on incoming data.

5.2. Natural Language Processing Integration

Natural Language Processing (NLP) is an important area of AI that enables machines to understand, interpret, and generate human language. By integrating NLP capabilities into your LangFlow agents, you can build intelligent systems capable of handling textual inputs, generating responses, and even learning from conversations.

LangFlow makes it easy to integrate NLP tools such as **spaCy**, **NLTK**, or **transformers** for tasks like text classification, entity recognition, and sentiment analysis.

For example, if you want to build an agent that can analyze the sentiment of customer feedback, you can use **Hugging Face's transformers** library with LangFlow as follows:

python

```python
from langflow import LangFlowAgent
from transformers import pipeline

# Initialize sentiment analysis pipeline
sentiment_analyzer = pipeline("sentiment-analysis")

# Define the agent
agent = LangFlowAgent(name="SentimentAnalysisAgent")

# Define the workflow for sentiment analysis
@agent.workflow
def analyze_sentiment(text: str) -> str:
    result = sentiment_analyzer(text)
    sentiment = result[0]['label']
    return f"The sentiment of the text is: {sentiment}"
```

```
if __name__ == "__main__":
    feedback = "I absolutely love this product!"
    response = agent.analyze_sentiment(feedback)
    print(response)
```

Explanation: This example uses the **Hugging Face Transformers** pipeline for sentiment analysis. The agent takes in a text input, processes it through the sentiment-analysis pipeline, and returns whether the sentiment is positive or negative.

Integrating NLP into AI agents opens up several powerful use cases:

- **Chatbots and Virtual Assistants**: Build conversational agents that can understand and respond to customer queries.
- **Text Classification**: Categorize documents or messages into predefined labels (e.g., spam detection, sentiment analysis).
- **Named Entity Recognition (NER)**: Extract specific entities (such as names, dates, and locations) from text.
- **Language Translation**: Translate text from one language to another using machine translation models.

NLP capabilities enhance the versatility and intelligence of your AI agents, making them much more capable in handling real-world data.

5.3. Implementing Custom Logic and Algorithms

While machine learning models and NLP capabilities are essential for many tasks, you may often need to implement custom logic and algorithms for more specialized functions. LangFlow allows you to write custom scripts and algorithms that can be seamlessly integrated into your AI agent's workflow.

LangFlow enables you to write custom logic in Python, which can be incorporated into workflows as reusable nodes. For instance, suppose you want to create an agent that processes user input and applies a custom business rule.

Here's an example of a custom algorithm that processes user queries and checks for certain keywords:

python

```python
from langflow import LangFlowAgent

# Define the agent
agent = LangFlowAgent(name="KeywordCheckAgent")

# Custom script for checking keywords
@agent.workflow
def check_keywords(query: str) -> str:
    important_keywords = ["urgent", "priority", "asap"]

    if any(keyword in query.lower() for keyword in important_keywords):
        return "This is a priority query."
    else:
        return "This is a regular query."

if __name__ == "__main__":
    query = "This issue is urgent, please help!"
    response = agent.check_keywords(query)
    print(response)
```

Explanation: This script checks if certain keywords are present in the user query (e.g., "urgent", "priority", or "asap"). If any of these keywords are found, the agent flags the query as a priority; otherwise, it processes it as a regular query.

As your custom logic grows more complex, it's important to optimize its performance:

- **Use Efficient Algorithms**: Ensure that your algorithms are time-efficient and space-efficient. For example, use **hashing** for faster lookups instead of linear searches.
- **Avoid Redundancy**: If your agent performs the same operation multiple times, try to cache the results to avoid unnecessary recalculations.
- **Parallel Processing**: For resource-heavy tasks, consider using multi-threading or multi-processing to run parts of the algorithm concurrently.

5.4. Optimizing AI Agent Performance

Optimizing your AI agent is essential for improving its efficiency and scalability, especially when working with large datasets or handling multiple requests simultaneously. LangFlow offers several strategies to optimize the performance of your agent and workflows.

To optimize performance, you first need to understand how your agent is performing. LangFlow provides tools to monitor key performance metrics:

- **Execution Time**: Track how long each workflow or node takes to execute.
- **Memory Usage**: Monitor the amount of memory consumed by your agent.
- **Error Rate**: Measure how often errors occur during execution.

- **Throughput**: Track how many tasks or requests your agent can handle per unit of time.

Here's how you can implement basic performance monitoring in LangFlow:

python

```python
import time
from langflow import LangFlowAgent

agent = LangFlowAgent(name="PerformanceMonitorAgent")

@agent.workflow
def monitor_performance(query: str) -> str:
    start_time = time.time()

    # Simulate processing time
    time.sleep(2)  # Simulate a delay (e.g., API call or data processing)

    execution_time = time.time() - start_time
    print(f"Execution time: {execution_time:.2f} seconds")

    return f"Processed query: {query}"

if __name__ == "__main__":
    query = "How are you?"
    response = agent.monitor_performance(query)
    print(response)
```

Explanation: In this example, the monitor_performance workflow tracks the execution time of a task by recording the start and end time. This can be expanded to monitor other metrics such as memory usage.

- **Asynchronous Processing**: For tasks that involve I/O operations (like API calls), use asynchronous processing to prevent blocking the agent's main workflow.
- **Caching**: Cache results of expensive computations or repeated tasks to speed up processing.
- **Load Balancing**: Distribute tasks across multiple instances of your agent to balance the load and improve responsiveness.

5.5. Managing AI Agent Dependencies

AI agents often rely on external libraries and services, which can create challenges when managing dependencies. LangFlow provides tools to help you handle dependencies and ensure that your AI agent runs smoothly across different environments.

Here are some best practices for managing dependencies in LangFlow:

- **Use Virtual Environments**: Always create a separate virtual environment for each project to isolate dependencies and avoid conflicts between different libraries.
- **Use requirements.txt**: Keep track of your agent's dependencies in a requirements.txt file, which can be used to install all necessary libraries at once.

bash

```
pip freeze > requirements.txt
```

- **Pin Dependency Versions**: Specify the exact versions of dependencies to avoid compatibility issues.

txt

```
langflow==2.0.1
tensorflow==2.6.0
```

When managing dependencies, it's important to handle version control efficiently. LangFlow helps you keep track of which versions of libraries are being used. Use **Git** to manage version control for your LangFlow projects, and commit your changes regularly.

- **Commit Best Practices**: Write clear commit messages that describe the purpose of the changes.
- **Branching Strategy**: Use feature branches for new development work and maintain a stable main branch for production-ready code.

In this chapter, we've explored how to enhance LangFlow AI agents with machine learning models, integrate natural language processing (NLP), and implement custom logic and algorithms. Additionally, we've discussed how to optimize the performance of your agent and manage dependencies effectively. By applying these advanced techniques, you can create intelligent, efficient, and scalable AI agents using LangFlow.

Chapter 6: Designing Robust Workflows

Designing robust workflows is one of the most important tasks when building AI agents in LangFlow. A well-architected workflow ensures that your system is not only efficient and scalable but also easy to maintain and extend. This chapter will guide you through best practices for designing, optimizing, and maintaining workflows in LangFlow, including modularity, error handling, optimization, and version control.

6.1. Workflow Architecture and Best Practices

Workflows in LangFlow consist of interconnected steps that define how data is processed. A solid workflow architecture ensures that your AI agent performs optimally, handles edge cases, and remains flexible to accommodate future needs.

When designing workflows, scalability should be a top priority. A scalable workflow can handle increasing amounts of data, user requests, or agent tasks without compromising performance.

Here are some key principles to consider when designing scalable workflows:

- **Decouple Components**: Each task in your workflow should be independent. This allows individual components to be scaled independently based on demand. For example, if data processing is a bottleneck, you can scale that part of the workflow without affecting other components.
- **Parallel Processing**: Workflows that perform tasks sequentially can be slow and inefficient. If tasks are independent, consider parallelizing them to reduce overall execution time. LangFlow supports asynchronous tasks and multi-threading to handle parallel processing efficiently.
- **Distributed Systems**: For large-scale applications, consider distributing tasks across multiple machines or containers. This

ensures that your workflow can handle high-volume data processing or computation-heavy tasks.

Example of a simple scalable workflow:

python

```python
from langflow import LangFlowAgent

# Define the agent
agent = LangFlowAgent(name="ScalableAgent")

@agent.workflow
def process_data_in_parallel(data):
    # Task 1 (can run independently)
    task1 = async_process_data_part1(data)

    # Task 2 (can run independently)
    task2 = async_process_data_part2(data)

    # Wait for both tasks to complete and aggregate results
    return await aggregate_results(task1, task2)
```

Explanation: In this example, two independent tasks are processed in parallel using async_process_data_part1 and async_process_data_part2. The results are aggregated once both tasks are complete, improving the overall speed and scalability of the workflow.

There are several common architectural patterns that can help structure your workflows, especially as complexity grows:

- **Pipeline Pattern**: This is the most common pattern in data processing workflows. It involves a linear series of processing steps, where the output of one step serves as the input for the next. For example, data might go through a pipeline of data cleaning, feature extraction, and model inference.
- **Event-Driven Pattern**: In this pattern, the workflow responds to specific events or triggers, such as receiving data from an external service or user input. Event-driven workflows are useful when you need to handle real-time data or notifications.
- **Map-Reduce Pattern**: For workflows that involve large datasets, the map-reduce pattern is ideal. In this pattern, data is split into smaller chunks (map phase), processed in parallel, and then the results are aggregated (reduce phase).

6.2. Creating Modular and Reusable Workflow Components

Modular workflows are easier to maintain, extend, and debug. By breaking down a large workflow into smaller, reusable components (or nodes), you can make the system more manageable and adaptable to future changes.

To design modular workflows, follow these best practices:

- **Single Responsibility**: Each component or node in a workflow should have one clear purpose. For example, a node should either clean data, transform it, or handle API requests, but not all of them at once.
- **Loose Coupling**: Keep components loosely coupled so that changes in one module do not affect others. This reduces the likelihood of bugs and makes the system more flexible.
- **Reusability**: Design components that can be reused across different workflows. For example, a common data transformation module that normalizes text can be used in multiple workflows without modification.

To create reusable modules, you can define individual workflow components (or nodes) as functions or classes that can be imported and used across different workflows.

Example of a reusable module for text preprocessing:

python

```python
# reusable_module.py

def clean_text(text: str) -> str:
    # Remove unnecessary whitespace and lowercase the text
    cleaned_text = text.strip().lower()
    return cleaned_text
```

In another workflow, you can import and use this module:

python

```python
from langflow import LangFlowAgent
from reusable_module import clean_text

agent = LangFlowAgent(name="TextCleanerAgent")

@agent.workflow
def preprocess_text(input_text: str) -> str:
    cleaned_text = clean_text(input_text)
    return cleaned_text
```

Explanation: The clean_text function is defined separately in a module called reusable_module.py and can be imported and used in multiple workflows without modification. This promotes code reuse and reduces redundancy.

6.3. Error Handling and Exception Management

Proper error handling and exception management are critical to building robust workflows. A well-designed error-handling system helps the agent recover from unexpected conditions and ensures that workflows can continue smoothly.

To handle errors effectively:

- **Anticipate Common Errors**: Consider potential issues such as invalid data types, missing values, or external service failures. Anticipating errors allows you to handle them before they cause a system crash.
- **Graceful Recovery**: When an error occurs, ensure that the system can recover gracefully. For instance, provide default fallback behaviors or retry logic when an external service fails.
- **Logging**: Log errors to help with debugging and monitoring. Logs provide a history of issues, which can be invaluable when troubleshooting.

Example of error handling in a LangFlow agent:

python

```python
from langflow import LangFlowAgent
import logging

# Set up logging
logging.basicConfig(level=logging.DEBUG)

agent = LangFlowAgent(name="ErrorHandlingAgent")
```

```python
@agent.workflow
def process_data(data):
    try:
        # Simulate a potential error in processing
        result = data["value"] * 10
    except KeyError as e:
        logging.error(f"KeyError: {e}")
        return "Error: Missing expected data field."
    except Exception as e:
        logging.error(f"Unexpected error: {e}")
        return "An unexpected error occurred."

    return result
```

Explanation: In this example, the workflow handles two types of errors: a KeyError when a required key is missing from the data, and a generic Exception for any other unexpected issues. The errors are logged for troubleshooting, and a user-friendly error message is returned.

- **Use Specific Exceptions**: Catch specific exceptions instead of a generic Exception. This allows you to handle different types of errors in tailored ways.
- **Provide Helpful Error Messages**: Ensure that the error messages returned to users or logs are clear and actionable.
- **Retry Logic**: For temporary issues, such as network errors, implement retry logic to attempt the action again after a brief delay.

6.4. Workflow Optimization Techniques

Optimizing workflows is essential for ensuring that your LangFlow agents perform efficiently, especially when handling large datasets or performing complex operations.

To streamline workflows, focus on reducing unnecessary steps, eliminating redundant operations, and leveraging asynchronous processing when appropriate. Here are a few techniques:

- **Remove Unnecessary Steps**: Evaluate your workflow to identify any unnecessary steps that don't add value to the end result.
- **Optimize Data Handling**: Use efficient data structures (like Pandas DataFrames or NumPy arrays) to store and process large datasets.
- **Batch Processing**: If possible, group tasks into batches to process them together rather than individually, which can improve efficiency.

Bottlenecks can slow down workflows significantly. Identifying and addressing them is key to improving performance. Here are some strategies:

- **Asynchronous Tasks**: For tasks like API calls or long-running computations, use asynchronous processing to prevent blocking other parts of the workflow.
- **Optimize API Calls**: Reduce the number of API calls by caching results or batching requests. Additionally, make sure API calls are made efficiently to minimize waiting times.
- **Load Balancing**: If your workflow is deployed across multiple instances or services, use load balancing to distribute tasks evenly and prevent any one instance from being overwhelmed.

6.5. Version Control for Workflows

Managing changes to your workflows is essential, especially when multiple developers are involved or when workflows evolve over time. Version control helps track changes and ensures that the most up-to-date version of the workflow is always in use.

Git is a widely used version control system, and LangFlow workflows can easily be integrated with Git to track changes over time.

To integrate Git with your LangFlow project:

Initialize a Git repository in your project directory:
bash

```
git init
```

Add files to the staging area:
bash

```
git add .
```

Commit changes to the repository:
bash

```
git commit -m "Initial commit of LangFlow workflows"
```

Push to a remote repository (e.g., GitHub):
bash

```
git push origin master
```

This allows you to track changes to your workflows, revert to previous versions, and collaborate effectively with other team members.

When working with multiple versions of a workflow, it's important to maintain clear versioning. A common practice is to append version numbers to workflow files and include them in your Git commits. For example:

- workflow_v1.py
- workflow_v2.py

Additionally, if changes to workflows are significant, use Git tags to label versions:

bash

```bash
git tag -a v1.0 -m "Initial version of workflow"
git push origin v1.0
```

This chapter has provided you with an in-depth guide to designing, optimizing, and managing robust workflows in LangFlow. By following these best practices for modularity, error handling, performance optimization, and version control, you can create efficient, maintainable, and scalable workflows that power your AI agents.

Chapter 7: Data Handling and Processing

Data handling and processing are fundamental to building effective AI agents and workflows in LangFlow. AI systems often require data from various sources, and this data needs to be processed, stored, and retrieved efficiently. This chapter will cover key topics such as data ingestion, transformation, storage, and real-time processing, as well as how to integrate databases seamlessly with LangFlow.

7.1. Data Ingestion Methods

Data ingestion is the process of collecting and importing data from various sources into your system for processing. Understanding how to efficiently ingest data is crucial for building scalable AI systems.

Data can come from various sources, each with different formats and access methods. Common data sources include:

- **APIs**: Many applications expose data via RESTful APIs or GraphQL. These APIs can provide structured data in JSON or XML format, often used for real-time or batch data ingestion.
- **Databases**: Data can be ingested from traditional SQL databases (e.g., MySQL, PostgreSQL) or NoSQL databases (e.g., MongoDB, Cassandra) using connectors or direct queries.
- **Files**: Data might be stored in files such as CSV, Excel, JSON, or XML. These files can be stored locally or remotely and can be ingested using file handling libraries.
- **Streams**: Real-time data, such as sensor readings, logs, or social media feeds, can be ingested through streaming platforms like **Apache Kafka** or **AWS Kinesis**.
- **Web Scraping**: Web scraping tools like **BeautifulSoup** or **Scrapy** can be used to extract structured data from websites.

Here is an example of ingesting data from a JSON API using Python's requests library:

python

```python
import requests

# Define the API endpoint
url = "https://api.example.com/data"

# Send GET request to fetch data
response = requests.get(url)

# Parse the JSON data
data = response.json()
print(data)
```

Explanation: In this example, the requests library is used to fetch data from a JSON API endpoint. The response is parsed and stored in the data variable for further processing.

There are several methods for ingesting data depending on the source and requirements:

- **Batch Processing**: Data is collected and processed in batches, typically for offline analysis. This method is appropriate when dealing with large datasets that can be processed in chunks.
- **Real-Time Processing**: Data is ingested and processed in real time as it becomes available. This is suitable for applications like monitoring, fraud detection, and recommendation systems.
- **Pull vs Push Models**: In the pull model, data is retrieved periodically from a source (e.g., scheduled API calls). In the push model, data is sent to the system as it's generated (e.g., webhooks, streaming services).

LangFlow supports integrating different ingestion methods into workflows, allowing for flexible data collection and processing strategies.

7.2. Data Transformation and Cleaning

Once data is ingested, it usually needs to be transformed and cleaned before it can be used by your AI agent. This process, often referred to as **ETL** (Extract, Transform, Load), ensures that the data is in the right format, free from errors, and consistent for further processing.

The ETL process consists of three main steps:

- **Extract**: Data is gathered from various sources (APIs, databases, files, etc.).
- **Transform**: The extracted data is cleaned, normalized, and formatted into a structure suitable for further analysis or machine learning.
- **Load**: The transformed data is loaded into a storage system (database, data warehouse, etc.).

Here is a simple Python example of an ETL pipeline that reads data from a CSV file, processes it, and saves the cleaned data to another file:

python

```python
import pandas as pd

# Step 1: Extract - Read data from CSV
data = pd.read_csv('raw_data.csv')

# Step 2: Transform - Clean and normalize data
```

```
data_cleaned = data.dropna()  # Remove rows with missing
values
data_cleaned.columns = [col.lower() for col in
data_cleaned.columns]  # Standardize column names


# Step 3: Load - Save the cleaned data to a new CSV file
data_cleaned.to_csv('cleaned_data.csv', index=False)
```

Explanation: This simple ETL pipeline reads data from a CSV file, removes rows with missing values (dropna()), and standardizes the column names to lowercase. The cleaned data is then saved to a new file. This process can be customized based on your specific needs (e.g., handling duplicates, scaling numerical data).

Effective data cleaning ensures that your AI models work with high-quality data. Common strategies include:

- **Handling Missing Values**: Decide how to treat missing values—either by removing rows with missing data or imputing values based on the data distribution.
- **Removing Duplicates**: Duplicate entries can skew analysis and machine learning models. Use techniques like drop_duplicates() to remove redundant data.
- **Outlier Detection**: Outliers can distort results, especially in machine learning. Methods like Z-score or IQR (Interquartile Range) can be used to detect and handle outliers.
- **Standardizing Data**: Ensure that data follows a consistent format (e.g., converting all text to lowercase, removing extra spaces).

7.3. Storing and Retrieving Data

Efficient data storage and retrieval are key to ensuring that your workflows run smoothly, especially when handling large datasets.

LangFlow supports integration with various data storage solutions to meet different project needs.

LangFlow can easily integrate with both SQL and NoSQL databases for storing and retrieving data. SQL databases are ideal for structured data that can be organized into tables, while NoSQL databases are more suitable for unstructured or semi-structured data.

Example of connecting to a SQL database (MySQL) using Python:

python

```python
import mysql.connector

# Connect to MySQL database
db_connection = mysql.connector.connect(
    host="localhost",
    user="your_username",
    password="your_password",
    database="your_database"
)

cursor = db_connection.cursor()

# Retrieve data from a table
cursor.execute("SELECT * FROM customers")
result = cursor.fetchall()

# Process the data
for row in result:
    print(row)
```

```
cursor.close()
db_connection.close()
```

Explanation: This code demonstrates how to connect to a MySQL database using mysql.connector, retrieve data from the customers table, and print the results.

There are several options for storing data, depending on your needs:

- **Relational Databases** (e.g., MySQL, PostgreSQL): Best for structured data with relationships between entities (e.g., customer data, transactions).
- **NoSQL Databases** (e.g., MongoDB, Cassandra): Ideal for unstructured or semi-structured data like JSON, text, or log files.
- **Cloud Storage** (e.g., AWS S3, Google Cloud Storage): Suitable for storing large volumes of data that need to be accessed by multiple services.
- **Data Lakes and Warehouses** (e.g., Amazon Redshift, Snowflake): These solutions are optimized for storing large-scale datasets and supporting analytics workflows.

LangFlow allows easy integration with these storage solutions, enabling efficient data management within your workflows.

7.4. Integrating Databases with LangFlow

LangFlow supports seamless integration with databases, allowing your AI agents to interact with data stored in SQL and NoSQL databases. Whether you're using structured data in a relational database or unstructured data in a NoSQL database, LangFlow can help you connect to these systems and perform data operations.

Connecting to an SQL Database:

LangFlow provides tools to connect to SQL databases using Python libraries like mysql.connector, psycopg2 (for PostgreSQL), or sqlalchemy.

Example of connecting to PostgreSQL using psycopg2:

python

```python
import psycopg2

# Connect to PostgreSQL database
conn = psycopg2.connect(
    dbname="your_database",
    user="your_username",
    password="your_password",
    host="localhost"
)

cursor = conn.cursor()

# Query data
cursor.execute("SELECT * FROM products")
products = cursor.fetchall()

# Print the data
for product in products:
    print(product)

cursor.close()
conn.close()
```

Explanation: This example shows how to connect to a PostgreSQL database, execute a query, and retrieve data. LangFlow can use this data in workflows for further processing.

Connecting to a NoSQL Database (MongoDB):

LangFlow can also interact with NoSQL databases like MongoDB, using Python libraries such as pymongo.

Example of connecting to MongoDB:

python

```python
from pymongo import MongoClient

# Connect to MongoDB
client = MongoClient("mongodb://localhost:27017/")
db = client["your_database"]

# Retrieve data from a collection
collection = db["your_collection"]
data = collection.find()

# Process the data
for record in data:
    print(record)
```

Explanation: In this example, the pymongo library is used to connect to a MongoDB database, retrieve documents from a collection, and print them.

To interact with databases, you can perform operations such as:

- **CRUD Operations**: Create, Read, Update, and Delete operations for managing database records.
- **Transactions**: Ensure data integrity by using transactions when performing multiple operations that must all succeed or fail together.
- **Indexing**: Use indexing to improve query performance, especially when dealing with large datasets.

7.5. Real-Time Data Processing

Real-time data processing is crucial for applications that require immediate decision-making or responses, such as fraud detection, live data analytics, or monitoring systems.

LangFlow supports integrating with real-time data streams using tools like **Apache Kafka**, **AWS Kinesis**, or **Apache Flink**. These tools allow you to process incoming data in real-time, providing up-to-date information for decision-making.

Example of setting up a simple real-time data processing pipeline using **Kafka**:

python

```python
from kafka import KafkaConsumer

# Create a Kafka consumer
consumer = KafkaConsumer(
    'your_topic',
    bootstrap_servers='localhost:9092',
    group_id='your_consumer_group'
)

# Process incoming messages
```

```
for message in consumer:
    print(f"Received message: {message.value.decode('utf-8')}")
```

Explanation: This example uses the KafkaConsumer class from the kafka-python library to listen to messages from a Kafka topic. It processes each incoming message and prints the result.

To handle real-time data effectively, consider the following techniques:

- **Event-Driven Architecture**: Implement event-driven architectures where workflows are triggered by specific events, such as receiving new data or detecting an anomaly.
- **Stream Processing Frameworks**: Use frameworks like **Apache Kafka**, **Apache Flink**, or **Apache Storm** for processing and analyzing data streams in real-time.
- **Message Queues**: Use message queues like **RabbitMQ** or **Kafka** to buffer data and ensure reliable delivery between different components of your workflow.

By integrating these tools with LangFlow, you can build powerful real-time data processing workflows that react to events instantly.

This chapter has covered the fundamental aspects of **data handling and processing**, from ingesting data from various sources to transforming, cleaning, storing, and retrieving data. Additionally, we've discussed how to integrate databases and implement real-time data processing in LangFlow, providing a comprehensive guide to managing data in your AI workflows.

Chapter 8: Integrating LangFlow with External Services

Integrating LangFlow with external services is crucial for expanding the capabilities of your AI agents and workflows. Whether you're connecting to RESTful APIs, setting up event-driven webhooks, or using third-party services like AWS or Google Cloud, understanding how to integrate these systems with LangFlow will allow your workflows to interact with a wider array of tools and services. This chapter provides comprehensive guidance on connecting LangFlow to external services, handling data from APIs, and ensuring secure, efficient interactions.

8.1. Connecting to RESTful APIs

RESTful APIs are widely used for providing and consuming data over the web. LangFlow allows easy integration with these APIs, enabling your workflows to interact with external services, retrieve data, and perform actions based on that data.

To connect LangFlow with a RESTful API, you'll typically need to send HTTP requests (e.g., GET, POST, PUT) to the API's endpoint, and process the responses.

Here's how to integrate a RESTful API into your LangFlow workflow:

Install the Requests Library: If you're working with Python, the requests library is a great tool for handling HTTP requests. Install it using pip if you haven't already:
bash

```
pip install requests
```

1.
2. **Define the API Integration**: In your LangFlow workflow, you can send a GET or POST request to an external API, process the response, and use that data for further operations.

Example of a GET request to a REST API:

python

```python
import requests
from langflow import LangFlowAgent

# Define the agent
agent = LangFlowAgent(name="APIIntegrationAgent")

@agent.workflow
def get_weather(city: str) -> str:
    api_url = f"http://api.weatherapi.com/v1/current.json?key=YOUR_API_KEY&q={city}"

    # Send a GET request to the weather API
    response = requests.get(api_url)

    # Check if the response was successful
    if response.status_code == 200:
        weather_data = response.json()
        temperature = weather_data['current']['temp_c']
        return f"The current temperature in {city} is {temperature}°C."
    else:
        return "Failed to retrieve weather data."

if __name__ == "__main__":
    city_name = "London"
    result = agent.get_weather(city_name)
```

```
print(result)
```

Explanation: In this example, the get_weather function sends a GET request to a weather API to fetch the current temperature of a specified city. If the request is successful (status code 200), it processes the JSON response to extract the temperature and returns it. If the request fails, it returns a failure message.

When interacting with RESTful APIs, it's essential to handle responses correctly. Typically, API responses are in JSON format, but they could also be in XML or plain text. The key points to handle in API responses include:

- **Check the HTTP Status Code**: Always verify that the response status code indicates success (e.g., 200 for success). Handle different status codes (e.g., 404 for not found, 500 for server errors).
- **Parse the Data**: Use methods like response.json() for JSON data or response.text for plain text to extract and work with the data.
- **Error Handling**: Proper error handling ensures that your workflow doesn't break when an external service is unavailable or returns unexpected data.

8.2. Webhooks and Event-Driven Integrations

Webhooks allow external systems to send data to your system in real time, making them ideal for event-driven architectures. With LangFlow, you can set up webhooks to receive events and trigger workflows based on incoming data.

To set up a webhook in LangFlow, you'll need to:

1. Expose an endpoint on your system that can accept incoming HTTP requests.

2. Configure the external service to send data to this endpoint whenever a specific event occurs (e.g., a new user registers or a payment is made).

Example of setting up a simple webhook handler in Flask (a lightweight web framework for Python):

python

```python
from flask import Flask, request
from langflow import LangFlowAgent

# Initialize Flask app and LangFlow agent
app = Flask(__name__)
agent = LangFlowAgent(name="WebhookAgent")

@app.route('/webhook', methods=['POST'])
def handle_webhook():
    data = request.json  # Get the incoming JSON data from the webhook
    event_type = data.get("event")

    # Trigger a specific workflow based on the event type
    if event_type == "new_user":
        return agent.new_user_welcome(data)
    elif event_type == "payment_received":
        return agent.payment_confirmation(data)
    else:
        return "Event not recognized", 400

if __name__ == "__main__":
    app.run(debug=True, port=5000)
```

Explanation: This example sets up a simple webhook listener using Flask. The /webhook endpoint listens for incoming POST requests, processes the JSON payload, and triggers specific workflows based on the event_type (e.g., new_user or payment_received). LangFlow can then execute the appropriate agent workflow based on the event.

Event-driven architectures often rely on **event streams** to handle real-time data. For managing event streams in LangFlow, tools like **Apache Kafka** or **AWS Kinesis** are often used. These tools allow you to handle high volumes of events efficiently.

Example of setting up an event stream with Kafka:

python

```python
from kafka import KafkaProducer

# Initialize Kafka producer
producer = KafkaProducer(bootstrap_servers='localhost:9092')

# Send a message to the "events" topic
producer.send('events', b'{"event": "new_user", "user_id": 123}')
producer.flush()
```

Explanation: In this example, a Kafka producer sends a message containing an event (a new user registration) to a Kafka topic. LangFlow can then consume this event from the topic and trigger corresponding workflows.

8.3. Using GraphQL with LangFlow

GraphQL is a powerful query language for APIs that allows clients to request exactly the data they need. Unlike REST, where you're limited to predefined endpoints, GraphQL gives you more flexibility by allowing you to query multiple resources in a single request.

GraphQL APIs are organized around a graph of data and allow you to fetch specific fields or related objects efficiently. In LangFlow, you can integrate GraphQL APIs to fetch or manipulate data in your workflows.

Here's an example of using the requests library to interact with a GraphQL API in LangFlow. Suppose you want to fetch user data from a GraphQL API:

python

```python
import requests
from langflow import LangFlowAgent

# Define the GraphQL query
graphql_query = """
  query {
    user(id: 123) {
      name
      email
      age
    }
  }
"""
```

```python
# Send the query to the GraphQL endpoint
response = requests.post(
    'https://api.example.com/graphql',
    json={'query': graphql_query}
)

# Handle the response
if response.status_code == 200:
    data = response.json()
    user = data['data']['user']
    print(f"User Info: {user['name']}, {user['email']}, {user['age']}")
else:
    print("Failed to fetch user data.")
```

Explanation: This example sends a GraphQL query to fetch user data from a GraphQL API. The response is processed and the relevant fields are extracted. LangFlow workflows can use this data for further processing or decision-making.

8.4. Third-Party Service Integrations

LangFlow can be integrated with a wide variety of third-party services to expand the capabilities of your workflows. Services like **AWS**, **Google Cloud**, and other cloud platforms provide APIs that can be utilized for tasks such as storage, machine learning, and messaging.

LangFlow can integrate with services such as AWS S3, Google Cloud Storage, or AWS Lambda to process data, store files, or invoke serverless functions.

Example of integrating with AWS S3 using the **boto3** library to upload files:

python

```python
import boto3
from langflow import LangFlowAgent

# Initialize the S3 client
s3_client = boto3.client('s3')

# Define the agent
agent = LangFlowAgent(name="AWSS3Agent")

@agent.workflow
def upload_file_to_s3(file_path: str, bucket_name: str):
    try:
        s3_client.upload_file(file_path, bucket_name,
'uploaded_file.txt')
        return f"File uploaded to S3 bucket: {bucket_name}"
    except Exception as e:
        return f"Error uploading file: {str(e)}"
```

Explanation: In this example, LangFlow is used to upload a file to an S3 bucket on AWS using the boto3 library. The workflow receives the file path and bucket name, and attempts to upload the file to the specified S3 bucket.

- **Handle Rate Limiting**: Many third-party APIs impose rate limits. Implement backoff strategies or error handling to manage these limits effectively.

- **Use SDKs**: Many services provide SDKs (e.g., boto3 for AWS, google-cloud for Google Cloud) that simplify the integration process.
- **Monitor API Usage**: Track your API usage and monitor for any errors or issues. This will help you ensure smooth operation and prevent unexpected disruptions.

8.5. Authentication and Security for Integrations

When integrating with external services, security and authentication are critical to protect sensitive data and maintain the integrity of your workflows.

To ensure that API connections are secure, follow these best practices:

- **Use HTTPS**: Always use HTTPS for secure communication with external APIs.
- **API Keys**: Store API keys securely (e.g., using environment variables or secret management services) and never expose them in code.
- **IP Whitelisting**: Some services allow you to restrict API access based on IP addresses, adding an extra layer of security.

OAuth is a popular authentication protocol that allows your application to access third-party services on behalf of users. Many services, like Google, AWS, and GitHub, support OAuth for secure API access.

Here's an example of how you might implement OAuth 2.0 authentication for accessing a service:

python

```
from requests_oauthlib import OAuth2Session
```

```python
# Define OAuth credentials and endpoint
client_id = 'YOUR_CLIENT_ID'
client_secret = 'YOUR_CLIENT_SECRET'
authorization_base_url = 'https://example.com/oauth/authorize'
token_url = 'https://example.com/oauth/token'

# Create an OAuth session
oauth = OAuth2Session(client_id)

# Get authorization URL
authorization_url, state = oauth.authorization_url(authorization_base_url)

# Redirect user to authorization URL and get the authorization response
print(f'Please go to {authorization_url} and authorize access.')

# After user authorizes, they will be redirected to a callback URL with a code
redirect_response = input('Paste the full redirect URL here: ')

# Fetch the access token
oauth.fetch_token(token_url,
authorization_response=redirect_response,
client_secret=client_secret)

# Use the OAuth session to access protected resources
response = oauth.get('https://api.example.com/userinfo')
```

```
print(response.json())
```

Explanation: This example demonstrates how to implement OAuth 2.0 authentication using the requests_oauthlib library. After obtaining the access token, the OAuth session can be used to make authenticated requests to the API.

This chapter has explored the different ways you can integrate LangFlow with external services, from connecting to RESTful APIs to managing event-driven workflows, using GraphQL, integrating third-party services, and ensuring secure communication. These techniques will help you build powerful, interconnected workflows that can interact with the broader ecosystem of tools and services.

Chapter 9: Customizing LangFlow Components

Customizing LangFlow components is a key aspect of tailoring the framework to meet the specific needs of your AI workflows. Whether you're creating custom nodes, extending existing components, or automating tasks, LangFlow's flexibility allows developers to adapt the platform for a wide range of use cases. This chapter will provide a detailed guide on how to create custom components, extend built-in ones, and optimize LangFlow for your unique requirements.

9.1. Creating Custom Nodes

In LangFlow, nodes are the building blocks of workflows. Each node performs a specific task, such as data processing, making API calls, or triggering events. Sometimes, the built-in nodes may not meet your specific requirements. In these cases, you can create custom nodes that integrate seamlessly into your workflow.

When designing a custom node, it is essential to consider the functionality you want to implement. A custom node should have:

- **Input Parameters**: The data that the node will receive from the previous node in the workflow.
- **Output Data**: The results or transformed data that the node will pass to the next step in the workflow.
- **Execution Logic**: The code that defines what the node will do with the input data.

A simple custom node could be designed to process numerical data, perform calculations, and pass the results along. The following sections will walk you through the process of designing and implementing such a custom node.

Here is a step-by-step example of implementing a custom node in LangFlow:

1. **Define the Custom Node**: Create a Python class that represents the custom node. This class should extend LangFlow's Node class, which provides the basic structure for all nodes.

python

```python
from langflow import Node

class MultiplyByTwoNode(Node):
    def process(self, input_data):
        # Ensure input_data is numeric
        if isinstance(input_data, (int, float)):
            return input_data * 2
        else:
            raise ValueError("Input data must be a number.")
```

Explanation: In this example, the MultiplyByTwoNode class inherits from LangFlow's Node class and implements the process method. The process method is where the node's functionality is defined. Here, it multiplies the input data by 2, but only if the input is numeric.

2. **Integrating the Custom Node into a Workflow**: Now that the custom node is defined, you can use it in a LangFlow workflow by creating a new agent and referencing the node.

python

```python
from langflow import LangFlowAgent

# Define the agent
agent = LangFlowAgent(name="CustomNodeAgent")
```

```python
# Define a workflow using the custom node
@agent.workflow
def calculate(input_value):
    node = MultiplyByTwoNode()
    return node.process(input_value)

if __name__ == "__main__":
    result = agent.calculate(10)
    print(f"Processed result: {result}")
```

Explanation: This workflow uses the custom node (MultiplyByTwoNode) to process an input value. When the workflow is executed, it multiplies the input value (in this case, 10) by 2, and the result is printed.

9.2. Extending Existing Components

While creating custom nodes is important, sometimes it's more efficient to extend or modify existing LangFlow components to suit your needs. Extending built-in components allows you to leverage the power of LangFlow while adding your own functionality.

To modify an existing component, such as a data processing node or an API integration, you can subclass it and override its behavior.

For example, if you want to modify a built-in node for API interaction to include additional logging:

python

```python
from langflow.components import APIRequestNode
```

```python
import logging

class LoggingAPIRequestNode(APIRequestNode):
    def process(self, url, params):
        logging.info(f"Sending request to URL: {url} with parameters: {params}")
        response = super().process(url, params)
        logging.info(f"Received response: {response.status_code}")
        return response
```

Explanation: The LoggingAPIRequestNode extends the APIRequestNode class, which is part of LangFlow's built-in components. It adds logging functionality before and after sending the request. By calling super().process(), it retains the original behavior of the APIRequestNode while adding the logging capability.

You can also enhance the capabilities of built-in components. For instance, you may want to add retry logic to a network-related component to handle temporary failures in API calls.

python

```python
import time
from langflow.components import APIRequestNode

class RetryAPIRequestNode(APIRequestNode):
    def process(self, url, params, retries=3, delay=2):
        attempt = 0
        while attempt < retries:
            try:
                response = super().process(url, params)
```

```python
        if response.status_code == 200:
            return response
        else:
            raise Exception(f"Unexpected status code:
{response.status_code}")
    except Exception as e:
        attempt += 1
        logging.error(f"Error during request: {e}. Retrying
({attempt}/{retries})...")
        time.sleep(delay)
    raise Exception("Max retries reached. Failed to process
API request.")
```

Explanation: In this example, the RetryAPIRequestNode adds retry logic to handle failures when making API calls. If an API call fails, the workflow waits for a short delay before retrying, up to a maximum number of retries. This enhancement ensures that the workflow is more resilient to temporary issues.

9.3. Scripting and Automation within LangFlow

LangFlow allows you to automate repetitive tasks by using scripting and integrating automation tools. Automating repetitive tasks not only saves time but also ensures consistency across workflows.

You can integrate scripting languages like **Python** or **JavaScript** within LangFlow workflows. This allows you to execute custom scripts that automate complex logic, process data, or interact with external systems.

Here's an example of automating a repetitive data transformation task using Python:

python

```python
from langflow import LangFlowAgent

agent = LangFlowAgent(name="AutomationAgent")

@agent.workflow
def automate_transformation(input_data):
    # Example: Normalize and scale the data
    normalized_data = [(x - min(input_data)) / (max(input_data) - min(input_data)) for x in input_data]
    return normalized_data

if __name__ == "__main__":
    data = [10, 20, 30, 40, 50]
    transformed_data = agent.automate_transformation(data)
    print(f"Transformed Data: {transformed_data}")
```

Explanation: This workflow automates the normalization of a dataset by scaling the data to a range between 0 and 1. The automate_transformation function performs this transformation on the input data.

You can automate a variety of tasks within LangFlow, including:

- **Data Preprocessing**: Automatically clean, normalize, and transform data before passing it through your workflows.
- **API Calls**: Automate interactions with external APIs by scheduling regular requests or triggering them based on events.
- **File Handling**: Automate tasks like file uploads, downloads, and organizing files based on specific rules.

LangFlow's built-in scheduling and task management features can help automate these workflows at set intervals or trigger them based on specific conditions.

9.4. UI Customizations for Workflows

While LangFlow is primarily a backend framework, you can customize the user interface (UI) to enhance the experience for users interacting with your workflows, especially when workflows involve monitoring or manual intervention.

LangFlow allows you to build custom UIs for workflow management. You can use tools like **Flask, Django**, or even **Streamlit** to create a UI that interacts with your LangFlow workflows.

Here's an example of using **Flask** to create a simple web interface to trigger LangFlow workflows:

python

```python
from flask import Flask, render_template, request
from langflow import LangFlowAgent

# Initialize Flask app and LangFlow agent
app = Flask(__name__)
agent = LangFlowAgent(name="WebUIAgent")

@app.route('/')
def home():
    return render_template('index.html')

@app.route('/run_workflow', methods=['POST'])
```

```
def run_workflow():
    input_value = request.form['input_value']
    result = agent.some_workflow(input_value)  # Trigger
the LangFlow workflow
    return f"Workflow result: {result}"


if __name__ == "__main__":
    app.run(debug=True)
```

Explanation: This Flask app renders an HTML template and allows users to submit input through a form. When the form is submitted, it triggers a LangFlow workflow (some_workflow) and displays the result on the page.

To enhance user experience, consider the following:

- **Real-Time Feedback**: Provide real-time updates on the status of workflows, such as displaying progress bars or notifying users of task completion.
- **Visualizations**: Use charts, graphs, or tables to present processed data in a more digestible format. Libraries like **Matplotlib** or **Plotly** can help integrate visualizations into your UI.
- **Interactive Elements**: Include interactive elements, such as buttons or dropdown menus, to allow users to modify inputs dynamically and trigger different workflows based on their selections.

9.5. Best Practices for Custom Component Development

Developing custom components that are maintainable, efficient, and flexible is crucial for the long-term success of your LangFlow projects.

Following coding best practices ensures that your components are easy to understand, modify, and extend.

To maintain a consistent codebase, adhere to the following coding standards:

- **Follow PEP 8**: Python's PEP 8 guidelines provide standards for writing clean, readable code.
- **Consistent Naming Conventions**: Use descriptive names for classes, functions, and variables to make your code self-explanatory.
- **Comment Your Code**: Write clear comments that explain what each part of your code does, especially in complex sections. This will help future developers understand your work.
- **Type Annotations**: Use type annotations for function arguments and return values to improve readability and catch errors early.

To ensure your custom components remain maintainable:

- **Modularize Code**: Break down complex components into smaller, reusable modules. This reduces code duplication and makes the system easier to update.
- **Write Tests**: Implement unit tests and integration tests to verify that your custom components work as expected.
- **Version Control**: Use Git or another version control system to track changes to your components and ensure that modifications can be reviewed and reverted if necessary.

This chapter has explored how to customize LangFlow components to fit your specific needs. You've learned how to create custom nodes, extend existing components, automate tasks, and optimize the UI for better user interaction. By following best practices for development, you can ensure that your LangFlow projects are scalable, maintainable, and efficient.

Chapter 10: Deployment Strategies

Deploying LangFlow applications efficiently is crucial for ensuring that they can scale, remain robust, and operate seamlessly in real-world environments. This chapter covers a range of deployment strategies, including on-premises, cloud-based, and hybrid deployment models. We'll also explore containerization using Docker, deploying to cloud platforms such as AWS, Azure, and GCP, setting up CI/CD pipelines, and implementing monitoring and maintenance strategies post-deployment.

10.1. Deployment Options for LangFlow Applications

Choosing the right deployment model depends on factors such as scalability, cost, security, and infrastructure requirements. In LangFlow, you can deploy applications in various environments, each offering different benefits and challenges.

- **On-Premises Deployment**: This involves deploying LangFlow applications on physical hardware within your organization. It gives you full control over your infrastructure, security, and data. However, it can be costly in terms of hardware, maintenance, and scaling.
  Advantages:
    - Full control over hardware and data security.
    - Can be more cost-effective for large-scale, long-term operations.
    - Suitable for highly regulated industries where data privacy is critical.
- **Challenges**:
    - Requires management of hardware, networking, and security.
    - Difficult to scale quickly without significant investment in infrastructure.
    - Limited flexibility when handling dynamic or unpredictable workloads.

- **Cloud Deployment**: This model involves deploying LangFlow applications on public or private cloud platforms like **AWS**, **Azure**, or **Google Cloud Platform (GCP)**. Cloud platforms provide flexibility, scalability, and ease of use for deploying applications.
  Advantages:
    - Easy to scale based on demand, with pay-as-you-go pricing models.
    - Managed infrastructure, reducing the burden of hardware maintenance.
    - Wide array of services available, including AI, storage, databases, and networking.
- **Challenges**:
    - Potential concerns around data security and compliance with cloud providers.
    - Dependency on third-party providers for uptime and service availability.
    - Ongoing operational costs that can increase with scaling.

A **hybrid deployment** combines both on-premises and cloud infrastructure. This approach allows organizations to benefit from the control and security of on-premises systems while leveraging the scalability and flexibility of the cloud.

Example Use Cases:

- **Data Sensitivity**: Sensitive data can be kept on-premises, while less critical workloads or applications can run in the cloud.
- **Disaster Recovery**: Cloud services can be used as a backup or disaster recovery solution for on-premises applications.

LangFlow supports hybrid deployments by allowing easy integrations with cloud services and local infrastructure, giving organizations the flexibility to manage different parts of their application in the environment that best suits their needs.

10.2. Containerization with Docker

Containerization is a key technology for simplifying the deployment and management of LangFlow applications. **Docker**is one of the most popular tools for creating, managing, and running containers.

Containers are lightweight, portable units that package applications and their dependencies into isolated environments. Docker makes it easy to deploy LangFlow applications in a consistent way across different environments.

- **Docker Image**: A template used to create containers. It contains the application and all its dependencies.
- **Docker Container**: A running instance of a Docker image.
- **Dockerfile**: A text file that contains instructions for building a Docker image.

Basic Docker Workflow:

1. **Create a Dockerfile**: Define the environment in which your LangFlow application will run.
2. **Build the Docker Image**: Build an image from the Dockerfile.
3. **Run the Container**: Launch a container from the built image.

Here's an example Dockerfile for a LangFlow application:

dockerfile

```
# Use a base Python image
FROM python:3.8-slim

# Set the working directory inside the container
WORKDIR /app
```

```
# Copy the application files to the container
COPY . /app

# Install the required dependencies
RUN pip install --no-cache-dir -r requirements.txt

# Expose the port that the app will run on
EXPOSE 5000

# Define the command to run the LangFlow application
CMD ["python", "app.py"]
```

***Explanation*: In this Dockerfile:**

- We start with a Python base image.
- We set the working directory to /app.
- We copy the application files into the container.
- We install the necessary Python dependencies using pip install.
- We expose port 5000 for the app to be accessible.
- Finally, we define the command to run the LangFlow application.

Once the Dockerfile is defined, you can build the Docker image and create a container as follows:

Build the Docker Image:
bash

```
docker build -t langflow-app .
```

Run the Docker Container:
bash

```
docker run -d -p 5000:5000 langflow-app
```

Explanation: The docker build command creates an image with the name langflow-app, and the docker run command starts the container in detached mode (-d) and maps port 5000 of the container to port 5000 on the host machine.

10.3. Deploying to Cloud Platforms (AWS, Azure, GCP)

Cloud platforms provide various services and tools that can help you deploy LangFlow applications efficiently. Here, we'll explore how to deploy LangFlow to **AWS**, **Azure**, and **Google Cloud Platform (GCP)**.

AWS (Amazon Web Services):

- **Elastic Beanstalk**: AWS's PaaS solution allows you to deploy and manage LangFlow applications easily. You can upload your Dockerized application, and Elastic Beanstalk will handle scaling, load balancing, and monitoring.
  Steps:
  1. Install the AWS Elastic Beanstalk CLI.
  2. Create an elasticbeanstalk configuration file.
  3. Deploy using eb create and eb deploy.

Azure:

- **Azure App Service**: A fully managed platform for building and deploying web applications. It supports Docker and can easily deploy LangFlow applications.

Steps:
1. Create a Docker container on Azure.
2. Push the Docker image to Azure Container Registry (ACR).
3. Configure Azure App Service to use the container from ACR.

Google Cloud Platform (GCP):

- **Google Kubernetes Engine (GKE)**: Use GKE for orchestrating LangFlow applications with Kubernetes.
  Steps:
  1. Push the Docker image to Google Container Registry.
  2. Create a Kubernetes cluster using GKE.
  3. Deploy your LangFlow application using Kubernetes deployments.

Cloud deployments can incur ongoing costs, especially with scaling. To manage and optimize costs:

- **Use Auto-scaling**: Configure auto-scaling policies based on the load to ensure that you only pay for the resources you need.
- **Monitor Usage**: Use cloud monitoring tools (e.g., AWS CloudWatch, Azure Monitor) to track resource usage and identify areas for cost reduction.
- **Optimize Storage**: Use cost-effective storage solutions (e.g., Amazon S3, Google Cloud Storage) to store large volumes of data.

10.4. Continuous Integration and Continuous Deployment (CI/CD)

CI/CD pipelines automate the process of testing, building, and deploying applications. By integrating CI/CD into your LangFlow workflows, you ensure that your applications are always up-to-date and that new features or bug fixes are deployed seamlessly.

To set up CI/CD pipelines for LangFlow, use popular CI/CD tools such as **Jenkins**, **GitLab CI**, or **GitHub Actions**.

Example GitHub Actions Workflow:

yaml

```yaml
name: LangFlow CI/CD

on:
  push:
    branches:
      - main

jobs:
  build:
    runs-on: ubuntu-latest
    steps:
      - name: Checkout code
        uses: actions/checkout@v2

      - name: Set up Python
        uses: actions/setup-python@v2
        with:
          python-version: '3.8'

      - name: Install dependencies
        run: |
          python -m pip install --upgrade pip
```

```yaml
        pip install -r requirements.txt

    - name: Run tests
      run: |
        pytest

    - name: Build Docker image
      run: |
        docker build -t langflow-app .

    - name: Deploy to Cloud
      run: |
        # Command to deploy your application
        ./deploy.sh
```

Explanation: **This GitHub Actions workflow automates the following steps:**

1. Checks out the code from the main branch.
2. Sets up Python and installs dependencies.
3. Runs unit tests using pytest.
4. Builds a Docker image of the LangFlow application.
5. Deploys the application to the cloud (in this case, a deployment script deploy.sh is used).

CI/CD automates testing, building, and deployment, ensuring that code changes are quickly integrated into production. Common steps in the CI/CD pipeline include:

- **Automated Testing**: Run unit tests, integration tests, and performance tests to verify code quality.
- **Automatic Deployment**: Deploy applications automatically to staging or production environments after passing tests.

- **Versioning**: Automatically increment version numbers and tag releases in your version control system.

10.5. Monitoring and Maintenance Post-Deployment

Once your LangFlow application is deployed, ongoing monitoring and maintenance are essential to ensure it continues to perform well and meets business needs.

Effective monitoring provides insights into your application's health and performance. You can use the following tools:

- **Prometheus and Grafana**: For real-time application monitoring and creating dashboards to visualize performance metrics.
- **AWS CloudWatch**: For monitoring cloud resources, setting up alarms, and logging application events.
- **Google Cloud Monitoring**: For monitoring GCP resources, tracking usage, and setting up alerts.

Example of setting up basic logging in a LangFlow application:

python

```python
import logging

# Set up basic logging
logging.basicConfig(level=logging.INFO)

@agent.workflow
def some_workflow(input_data):
    logging.info(f"Processing input: {input_data}")
```

```python
# Processing logic here
result = input_data * 2
logging.info(f"Result: {result}")
return result
```

Explanation: This example uses Python's built-in logging module to log input data and results within the LangFlow workflow.

Routine maintenance ensures your application stays secure, optimized, and bug-free. Common tasks include:

- **Software Updates**: Regularly update dependencies and frameworks to keep your system secure and improve performance.
- **Backup and Recovery**: Implement automated backup strategies to safeguard critical data and ensure business continuity.
- **Security Audits**: Regularly audit your system for security vulnerabilities, especially if your application handles sensitive data.

This chapter has covered the essential deployment strategies for LangFlow applications, including on-premises, cloud, and hybrid deployment models. We've discussed containerization with Docker, deploying to major cloud platforms, setting up CI/CD pipelines, and monitoring and maintaining applications post-deployment. By using these deployment strategies, you can ensure that your LangFlow application is scalable, efficient, and secure in any environment.

Chapter 11: Security Best Practices

Security is an essential aspect of deploying AI agents and workflows. In this chapter, we will explore security best practices for LangFlow applications, focusing on how to secure AI agents and workflows, ensure data privacy, implement authentication and authorization, follow secure coding practices, and conduct regular security audits.

11.1. Securing AI Agents and Workflows

AI agents and workflows are often involved in handling sensitive data or interacting with external systems. As such, securing these components is critical to ensure they operate safely and protect both user data and system integrity.

To ensure the security of AI agents and workflows, several protocols should be implemented:

1. **Encryption**:
   - **Data Encryption**: Use encryption to protect data both in transit and at rest. This is especially important when dealing with sensitive data like personal information or financial transactions.
   - **TLS (Transport Layer Security)**: Use TLS for encrypting data transmitted over the network. Ensure that all communication between components, including API calls and database connections, is encrypted.

Example of Enabling HTTPS for an API:
python

```python
from flask import Flask
from OpenSSL import SSL

app = Flask(__name__)

context = SSL.Context(SSL.SSLv23_METHOD)
```

```python
context.use_certificate_file('path/to/cert.pem')
context.use_privatekey_file('path/to/key.pem')

@app.route('/')
def hello_world():
    return 'Hello, secure world!'

if __name__ == '__main__':
    app.run(ssl_context=context)
```

2. *Explanation:* This example sets up an HTTPS server in Flask using SSL certificates to encrypt data during communication. By enforcing HTTPS, we ensure that data transmitted between clients and the server is encrypted.
3. **API Authentication**:
    ○ **API Keys**: Use API keys to authenticate and authorize requests to external services. These keys should be stored securely, for example in environment variables or a secrets management tool.
    ○ **OAuth**: Implement OAuth for secure, token-based authentication when integrating with third-party services.

There are several common security threats that AI agents and workflows need to protect against:

1. **Injection Attacks**:
    ○ SQL injection and command injection are serious vulnerabilities where an attacker can insert malicious code into your system. To prevent these attacks, always use parameterized queries or ORM frameworks when interacting with databases.

Example (using parameterized SQL queries to prevent SQL injection):
python

```python
import mysql.connector
```

```python
conn = mysql.connector.connect(
    host="localhost",
    user="your_username",
    password="your_password",
    database="your_database"
)

cursor = conn.cursor()

# Safe query to prevent SQL injection
cursor.execute("SELECT * FROM users WHERE username
= %s", (username,))
result = cursor.fetchall()
```

2. *Explanation:* This example uses parameterized queries in MySQL, which helps prevent SQL injection by separating the query structure from user inputs.
3. **Cross-Site Scripting (XSS)**:
   - XSS occurs when an attacker injects malicious scripts into web applications. To prevent XSS, sanitize user inputs and avoid rendering untrusted content directly in HTML.

Example (escaping HTML input):
python

```python
from html import escape

user_input = "<script>alert('Hacked');</script>"
safe_input = escape(user_input)
print(safe_input)  # Output will be
"&lt;script&gt;alert('Hacked');&lt;/script&gt;"
```

4. *Explanation:* The escape() function from Python's html library is used to sanitize user input by escaping potentially harmful characters (like <, >, etc.) before rendering it on a webpage.

11.2. Data Privacy and Compliance

As AI systems increasingly handle personal data, adhering to data privacy and compliance regulations becomes crucial. It is essential to understand and implement the necessary privacy protocols to ensure that data is processed securely and in accordance with legal requirements.

Different regions have established data protection laws to safeguard individuals' privacy. For example:

- **GDPR (General Data Protection Regulation)**: This EU regulation governs how businesses collect, store, and process personal data. It mandates transparency, consent, and data subject rights (e.g., the right to access, rectification, and deletion).
- **CCPA (California Consumer Privacy Act)**: This regulation grants California residents rights over their personal data, including the ability to opt-out of data sales and request data deletion.
- **HIPAA (Health Insurance Portability and Accountability Act)**: This U.S. regulation sets standards for the protection of health information.

To ensure compliance with data protection laws, follow these guidelines:

- **Data Minimization**: Only collect and process the data you absolutely need for your workflows.
- **Consent Management**: Ensure that explicit consent is obtained from users before collecting or processing their personal data.
- **Data Anonymization**: Where applicable, anonymize or pseudonymize data to protect individual identities.
- **Access Control**: Ensure that data is only accessible to authorized individuals and systems.

Example of Implementing Data Access Control:

python

```python
# Example: Using RBAC (Role-Based Access Control) to
restrict access to sensitive data
from langflow import LangFlowAgent

# Define roles
admin_role = "admin"
user_role = "user"

# Define the agent
agent = LangFlowAgent(name="SecureAgent")

@agent.workflow
def view_sensitive_data(user_role):
    if user_role == admin_role:
        # Return sensitive data
        return "Sensitive Data"
    else:
        return "Access Denied"
```

Explanation: This workflow checks the user's role before providing access to sensitive data. Only users with the admin role can view the sensitive data.

11.3. Implementing Authentication and Authorization

Authentication and authorization are key components of application security. Authentication ensures that users are who they claim to be, while authorization controls what actions authenticated users can perform.

RBAC is a security model that assigns permissions to users based on their roles. Each role corresponds to a set of permissions that control access to different resources and workflows.

Example of Implementing RBAC in LangFlow:

python

```python
# Define roles and permissions
roles = {
    "admin": ["view_sensitive_data", "edit_data",
"delete_data"],
    "user": ["view_data"]
}

def check_permission(user_role, action):
    if action in roles.get(user_role, []):
        return True
    else:
        return False

# Check if a user has permission to perform an action
user_role = "user"
action = "edit_data"

if check_permission(user_role, action):
    print("Permission granted.")
else:
    print("Permission denied.")
```

Explanation: This code snippet defines roles and permissions for each role. The check_permission function checks if a user has permission to perform a specific action based on their role.

You can manage user permissions by defining roles and assigning specific access rights to them. Additionally, consider using OAuth,

JWT tokens, or third-party authentication services to secure user login and session management.

11.4. Secure Coding Practices in LangFlow

Writing secure code is one of the most effective ways to prevent security vulnerabilities. By adhering to secure coding practices, you can significantly reduce the risk of introducing exploitable flaws in your LangFlow applications.

Follow these best practices to write secure code in LangFlow:

- **Input Validation**: Always validate user inputs to ensure they meet expected formats. Use input sanitization and validation libraries to prevent malicious input.
- **Least Privilege**: Assign the minimum level of access required for a task. Ensure that your workflows only have access to the resources they absolutely need.
- **Use Secure Libraries**: Ensure that any third-party libraries or dependencies you use are secure and maintained. Avoid using outdated or unsupported libraries.

Common vulnerabilities in web applications include:

- **Buffer Overflow**: Ensure that inputs are bounded and checked to avoid buffer overflow attacks.
- **Cross-Site Request Forgery (CSRF)**: Implement anti-CSRF tokens to prevent unauthorized actions from being performed by malicious third parties.
- **Insecure Deserialization**: Avoid deserializing untrusted data, as it may lead to remote code execution vulnerabilities.

Example of Preventing CSRF in Flask:

python

```
from flask_wtf.csrf import CSRFProtect
```

```
app = Flask(__name__)
csrf = CSRFProtect(app)

@app.route('/submit', methods=['POST'])
def submit_form():
    return "Form submitted successfully."
```

Explanation: This example uses the **Flask-WTF** extension to protect against CSRF attacks by generating tokens that must be included with every form submission.

11.5. Regular Security Audits and Vulnerability Assessments

Security is an ongoing process. Regular security audits and vulnerability assessments help identify and mitigate potential weaknesses in your LangFlow applications.

A security audit involves reviewing your codebase, infrastructure, and workflows for security vulnerabilities. Here's how to conduct a basic audit:

- **Code Review**: Conduct periodic code reviews to ensure that security best practices are followed.
- **Static Analysis Tools**: Use static analysis tools like **SonarQube** or **Bandit** to automatically scan your code for common security issues.
- **Penetration Testing**: Simulate attacks on your system to identify vulnerabilities that may be exploited by hackers.

Once vulnerabilities are identified:

- **Patch Security Holes**: Apply patches or updates to libraries and frameworks that contain vulnerabilities.

- **Test Fixes**: After applying security fixes, test the application to ensure the fix resolves the issue without introducing new problems.
- **Monitor Systems**: Use monitoring tools to detect any unusual behavior that might indicate a security breach.

This chapter has covered essential security best practices for LangFlow applications, from securing AI agents and workflows to ensuring data privacy, implementing authentication, and writing secure code. Regular security audits and proper vulnerability assessments are vital to maintaining a secure environment for your LangFlow applications. By adhering to these best practices, you can mitigate risks and ensure the robustness and safety of your system.

Chapter 12: Scalability and Performance Optimization

Scalability and performance optimization are vital components of any AI system. LangFlow applications, like any AI-powered platform, must be designed to handle increasing amounts of data, users, or workloads without sacrificing performance. This chapter will cover various strategies to ensure that LangFlow workflows and AI agents scale efficiently and perform optimally, focusing on scalability concepts, load balancing, workflow optimization, resource management, and horizontal/vertical scaling.

12.1. Understanding Scalability in LangFlow

Scalability is the ability of a system to handle an increasing amount of work or its potential to accommodate growth. In LangFlow, scalability refers to the platform's ability to manage larger workflows, more complex AI models, and increasing data volumes as your application grows.

When discussing scalability, it's important to differentiate between different types of scalability:

- **Vertical Scaling (Scaling Up)**: This involves adding more resources (CPU, RAM, storage) to a single machine to handle more work. Vertical scaling is easier to implement but has its limits in terms of hardware upgrades.
- **Horizontal Scaling (Scaling Out)**: Horizontal scaling refers to adding more machines (or containers) to distribute the workload across multiple servers. This approach is more scalable than vertical scaling and can handle much larger loads.

Key principles of scalability include:

1. **Elasticity**: The system should be able to scale resources up or down based on demand. Cloud platforms like AWS, Azure, and GCP provide elastic scaling features.

2. **Load Distribution**: Distributing workloads efficiently across multiple systems ensures that no single machine or process becomes a bottleneck.
3. **Decoupling**: Modularizing workflows into independent components or services allows for easy scaling of individual parts of the system as needed.

Assessing the scalability requirements of your LangFlow application involves evaluating the expected traffic, data volume, and processing complexity. Here's how to assess scalability needs:

- **Traffic Prediction**: Estimate how much traffic your application is likely to handle in the future based on user growth, seasonality, and the nature of the application.
- **Data Growth**: Consider how data volume is expected to grow and how it will be processed and stored.
- **Complexity of AI Models**: Complex AI models (such as large language models or deep learning networks) often require more compute resources and may need to be scaled differently.

A simple example to monitor scalability could involve logging performance metrics like response time and CPU usage under load:

python

```python
import psutil

# Monitor CPU usage and memory consumption
cpu_usage = psutil.cpu_percent(interval=1)

memory_usage = psutil.virtual_memory().percent

print(f"CPU Usage: {cpu_usage}%")

print(f"Memory Usage: {memory_usage}%")
```

Explanation: This snippet uses the psutil library to monitor CPU and memory usage, helping you identify potential scalability issues under load.

12.2. Load Balancing Techniques

Load balancing is critical for ensuring that the workload is distributed evenly across servers or containers, preventing any single machine from becoming overwhelmed.

A load balancer distributes incoming network traffic across multiple servers, ensuring that no single server becomes a bottleneck. Popular load balancing solutions include **NGINX**, **HAProxy**, and **AWS Elastic Load Balancing**.

Example of setting up a simple load balancer using NGINX:

nginx

```
http {

  upstream backend {

    server backend1.example.com;

    server backend2.example.com;

  }


  server {

    listen 80;
```

```
    location / {

      proxy_pass http://backend;

    }

  }

}
```

Explanation: This NGINX configuration creates an upstream server pool that includes backend1.example.com and backend2.example.com. All incoming traffic is directed to one of these backend servers based on load-balancing algorithms.

When distributing workloads across multiple servers, consider the following strategies:

- **Round Robin**: Requests are distributed evenly across all servers. This is the default strategy for many load balancers.
- **Least Connections**: Requests are sent to the server with the fewest active connections. This can help balance the load based on the current demand.
- **Weighted Distribution**: Different servers can be assigned different weights depending on their processing power. Servers with higher processing power receive more traffic.

12.3. Optimizing Workflow Performance

Performance optimization ensures that LangFlow workflows execute efficiently and within a reasonable time frame, even as data volumes or complexity increase.

Identifying performance bottlenecks involves monitoring various parts of your workflow to detect which components are slowing down the system. Common bottlenecks include:

- **Data Processing**: Large datasets may cause slowdowns during preprocessing, especially if data transformations or feature engineering are involved.
- **AI Model Inference**: Running machine learning models, especially complex ones, can be time-consuming and resource-intensive.
- **Database Queries**: Inefficient database queries, particularly with large datasets, can slow down workflows.

Use profiling tools such as **cProfile** in Python to analyze where your workflow is spending most of its time:

python

```python
import cProfile

def process_data():
    # Data processing logic
    pass

cProfile.run('process_data()')
```

Explanation: This code snippet uses cProfile to profile the process_data() function. Profiling helps you understand where the most time is spent, allowing you to target optimizations.

Parallel Processing: For computationally intensive tasks, use multi-threading or multi-processing to parallelize data processing or model inference. Python's concurrent.futures or multiprocessing modules can help with parallelization.

Example:

python

```python
from concurrent.futures import ThreadPoolExecutor


def process_task(task):

    # Processing logic

    pass


tasks = ["task1", "task2", "task3"]

with ThreadPoolExecutor() as executor:

    executor.map(process_task, tasks)
```

1. *Explanation*: This example uses the ThreadPoolExecutor to process tasks concurrently, improving throughput by utilizing multiple threads.
2. **Caching**: Cache the results of expensive operations or frequent database queries to reduce computation time and improve performance. Tools like **Redis** or **Memcached** can be used for caching.
3. **Optimize Database Queries**: Use indexing, efficient joins, and pagination to speed up database operations.
4. **Asynchronous Processing**: Use asynchronous programming techniques to avoid blocking tasks, particularly when dealing with external API calls or I/O operations. Python's asyncio library can help with non-blocking operations.

12.4. Resource Management and Allocation

Proper resource management ensures that your LangFlow application makes efficient use of compute and storage resources, preventing waste and ensuring that your system can scale efficiently.

To optimize resource utilization:

- **Right-size your instances**: Choose the appropriate instance types based on the resource needs of your LangFlow agents and workflows.
- **Auto-scaling**: Configure auto-scaling policies based on workload demands to automatically adjust the number of resources allocated to the application.
- **Task Scheduling**: Schedule computationally expensive tasks to run during off-peak hours to optimize resource usage.

Example of configuring auto-scaling on AWS EC2:

json

```json
{

  "AutoScalingGroupName": "LangFlowGroup",

  "MinSize": 2,

  "MaxSize": 10,

  "DesiredCapacity": 4,

  "LaunchConfigurationName": "LangFlowLaunchConfig",

  "AvailabilityZones": ["us-west-2a", "us-west-2b"]

}
```

Explanation: This configuration defines an auto-scaling group in AWS, with a minimum of 2 instances and a maximum of 10. The system will scale the number of instances between these limits based on demand.

Efficient management of compute and storage resources is crucial for performance and cost optimization:

- **Compute Resources**: Use **containerization** (e.g., Docker) or **serverless architectures** (e.g., AWS Lambda) for efficient scaling and resource utilization.
- **Storage Resources**: Use distributed storage systems (e.g., **Amazon S3** or **Google Cloud Storage**) for large datasets and ensure that storage is appropriately partitioned and indexed.

12.5. Scaling AI Agents Horizontally and Vertically

When scaling AI agents, you can scale either horizontally (adding more instances) or vertically (adding more resources to a single instance). Both approaches have their strengths and weaknesses, and understanding when to use each one is key to building efficient, scalable systems.

- **Vertical Scaling**: Adding more CPU, RAM, or storage to an existing server. This is often the simplest approach, but it has physical limits. It is ideal for applications with limited scalability requirements.
  Pros:
    o Simpler to implement.
    o No need to manage multiple servers.
- **Cons**:
    o Limited by hardware capacity.
    o Increased risk of a single point of failure.

- **Horizontal Scaling**: Adding more instances or servers to distribute the load. This is suitable for large-scale applications that need to handle high volumes of data or traffic.
  Pros:
  - Can handle large workloads.
  - Fault tolerance (if one server fails, others can take over).
- **Cons**:
  - More complex to manage.
  - Requires load balancing.

To scale AI agents efficiently:

- **Use Microservices**: Break down the AI agent into smaller, independent microservices that can be scaled independently based on demand.
- **Deploy Using Containers**: Docker containers make it easy to scale AI agents horizontally by deploying multiple instances across different machines.
- **Use a Kubernetes Cluster**: For more complex systems, use Kubernetes to manage and orchestrate containers, ensuring automatic scaling and fault tolerance.

Example of deploying AI agents using Kubernetes:

yaml

```yaml
apiVersion: apps/v1

kind: Deployment

metadata:

  name: langflow-agent

spec:

  replicas: 3
```

```yaml
  selector:
    matchLabels:
      app: langflow-agent
  template:
    metadata:
      labels:
        app: langflow-agent
    spec:
      containers:
      - name: langflow-agent
        image: langflow-agent-image:latest
        ports:
        - containerPort: 5000
```

Explanation: This Kubernetes configuration deploys three replicas of the LangFlow agent, ensuring that the workload is distributed across multiple instances.

This chapter has explored the core concepts of scalability and performance optimization for LangFlow applications. We covered how to scale AI agents, implement load balancing, optimize workflows, manage resources, and scale horizontally and vertically. By applying these strategies, you can ensure that your LangFlow applications are capable of handling increasing workloads efficiently and effectively.

Chapter 13: Testing and Quality Assurance

Ensuring the quality and reliability of your LangFlow applications is essential to maintaining a high-performance system. Comprehensive testing and quality assurance (QA) practices help detect bugs, validate functionality, and ensure that your workflows and agents perform as expected. This chapter will explore how to implement unit tests, integration tests, automated testing, performance tests, and continuous quality improvement for LangFlow components.

13.1. Unit Testing LangFlow Components

Unit testing is a fundamental part of ensuring that individual components of your LangFlow application work as expected. Unit tests focus on testing the smallest parts of your application (such as individual functions or methods) in isolation.

To write effective unit tests for LangFlow components, follow these best practices:

- **Test Small Units of Code**: Write tests for individual functions, classes, or methods, ensuring that they perform the correct task.
- **Mock Dependencies**: If your component interacts with external services or databases, use mock objects to simulate those dependencies, ensuring that your tests are isolated and repeatable.
- **Test Edge Cases**: Include tests for boundary cases and invalid inputs to ensure that your components handle unexpected scenarios.

Example of Writing a Unit Test for a LangFlow Node:

python

```python
import unittest

from langflow import LangFlowAgent


# A simple LangFlow agent and workflow
class MultiplyByTwoNode:
    def process(self, input_data):
        if isinstance(input_data, (int, float)):
            return input_data * 2
        else:
            raise ValueError("Input data must be a number.")


class TestMultiplyByTwoNode(unittest.TestCase):

    def setUp(self):
        self.node = MultiplyByTwoNode()

    def test_process_valid_data(self):
        result = self.node.process(5)
        self.assertEqual(result, 10)

    def test_process_invalid_data(self):
```

```
    with self.assertRaises(ValueError):

        self.node.process("invalid")


if __name__ == "__main__":

    unittest.main()
```

Explanation: In this example, the MultiplyByTwoNode is tested using Python's built-in unittest framework. The test_process_valid_data test ensures that the node correctly multiplies a valid number by 2, while the test_process_invalid_data test checks that it raises a ValueError when the input is invalid.

Several tools and frameworks can help you write and run unit tests effectively:

- **unittest**: Python's built-in testing framework, which is simple and powerful for unit testing.
- **pytest**: A popular testing framework that supports more advanced features such as fixtures, parameterized tests, and better output formatting.
- **mock**: A Python library used to mock dependencies and isolate the components being tested.
- **nose2**: An extended version of the built-in unittest framework that offers additional features, such as test discovery.

13.2. Integration Testing for Workflows

Integration testing verifies that multiple components of the LangFlow workflow work together as expected. These tests focus on how different modules and services interact, ensuring that the overall system functions properly.

In integration tests, you typically simulate real interactions between components (e.g., database, APIs, or other services). The goal is to test the entire system's behavior under realistic conditions.

Example of Writing an Integration Test for a LangFlow Workflow:

python

```python
import unittest

from langflow import LangFlowAgent


# Mock component that simulates an external API call

class MockAPI:
    def fetch_data(self):
        return {"status": "success", "data": [1, 2, 3, 4]}


# LangFlow agent that integrates with the MockAPI

class DataProcessingAgent(LangFlowAgent):


    def __init__(self):
        super().__init__(name="DataProcessor")
        self.api = MockAPI()
```

```python
@LangFlowAgent.workflow
def process_data(self):
    data = self.api.fetch_data()
    return sum(data['data'])


class TestDataProcessingAgent(unittest.TestCase):

    def setUp(self):
        self.agent = DataProcessingAgent()

    def test_process_data(self):
        result = self.agent.process_data()
        self.assertEqual(result, 10)  # Sum of [1, 2, 3, 4]


if __name__ == "__main__":
    unittest.main()
```

Explanation: This integration test simulates how the DataProcessingAgent interacts with the MockAPI. The test checks if the process_data workflow correctly processes the data from the API. In this case, the test verifies that the sum of the data returned by the mock API is 10.

To ensure that components work seamlessly together, it's important to:

- **Mock External Services**: When your workflows rely on external services or APIs, mock those services to simulate real interactions without needing to hit live endpoints.
- **Test with Real Data**: Whenever possible, run integration tests with real or realistic data to ensure that all components behave as expected in a production-like environment.
- **Run End-to-End Tests**: Perform end-to-end tests that simulate the entire workflow, ensuring that all components work together correctly.

13.3. Automated Testing Frameworks

Automated testing is essential for continuous quality assurance in LangFlow applications. With automated tests, you can ensure that your workflows and agents behave as expected every time code changes are made, without manual intervention.

To set up automated tests, integrate your testing framework into your development pipeline. Use tools like **GitHub Actions**, **Jenkins**, or **GitLab CI** to automatically run tests whenever code is pushed or merged.

Example GitHub Actions Workflow for Automated Testing:

yaml

```
name: LangFlow CI


on:
```

```yaml
  push:
    branches:
      - main
  pull_request:
    branches:
      - main

jobs:
  test:
    runs-on: ubuntu-latest
    steps:
      - name: Checkout code
        uses: actions/checkout@v2

      - name: Set up Python
        uses: actions/setup-python@v2
        with:
          python-version: '3.8'

      - name: Install dependencies
        run: |
```

```
      python -m pip install --upgrade pip

      pip install -r requirements.txt


   - name: Run tests

     run: |

       pytest
```

Explanation: This GitHub Actions workflow automatically runs tests every time code is pushed to the main branch or a pull request is made. It installs dependencies, runs the tests using pytest, and ensures that your codebase remains stable.

Continuous testing is part of a broader DevOps culture that includes continuous integration and deployment (CI/CD). Best practices for continuous testing include:

- **Automate Tests for Every Change**: Every time new code is pushed or merged, automated tests should run to verify that nothing breaks.
- **Use a Dedicated Testing Environment**: Create isolated environments for running tests to ensure that they don't affect production systems.
- **Test Coverage**: Strive for high test coverage, especially for critical parts of the application, to minimize the risk of defects.

13.4. Performance Testing

Performance testing ensures that your LangFlow workflows and AI agents can handle expected loads without issues like high latency or crashes.

Load Testing simulates the expected number of concurrent users or requests to see how the system behaves under normal conditions. **Stress Testing** pushes the system beyond its limits to identify failure points and measure how it recovers.

Example of Load Testing with Python's Locust:

python

```python
from locust import HttpUser, task, between


class LangFlowUser(HttpUser):
    wait_time = between(1, 5)


    @task
    def process_workflow(self):
        self.client.get("/process_data")


if __name__ == "__main__":
    import locust
    locust.run()
```

Explanation: In this example, Locust is used for load testing the process_data endpoint of a LangFlow application. The script simulates multiple users sending GET requests to this endpoint and measures the response times.

Key performance metrics to monitor during performance testing include:

- **Response Time**: The time it takes for the system to respond to a request.
- **Throughput**: The number of requests processed by the system in a given period.
- **Error Rate**: The percentage of requests that result in errors.
- **Resource Utilization**: Metrics such as CPU, memory, and disk usage during testing.

You can use monitoring tools like **Prometheus**, **Grafana**, or cloud-specific solutions like **AWS CloudWatch** to gather and visualize these metrics.

13.5. Continuous Quality Improvement

Continuous quality improvement (CQI) is an ongoing process aimed at ensuring that the quality of your LangFlow application improves over time. This involves integrating feedback, optimizing workflows, and improving testing practices.

To implement a robust QA process:

- **Test Early and Often**: Start testing early in the development process and run tests frequently to catch issues early.
- **Automate QA**: Automate as much of the QA process as possible, including testing, deployment, and monitoring.
- **Peer Reviews**: Conduct code reviews to ensure that best practices are followed and that the codebase remains maintainable and secure.

Feedback loops are essential to continuous improvement. You can leverage feedback from various sources to refine your LangFlow application:

- **User Feedback**: Gather user feedback on application performance and usability to identify areas for improvement.
- **Monitoring Insights**: Use metrics from performance and load testing to identify bottlenecks and optimize workflows.
- **Bug Reports**: Prioritize addressing bugs or issues identified by users or automated tests to maintain system stability.

This chapter has explored how to implement testing and quality assurance for LangFlow applications. We've covered unit testing, integration testing, automated testing frameworks, performance testing, and continuous quality improvement practices. By incorporating these practices, you can ensure that your LangFlow applications remain reliable, performant, and of the highest quality.

Chapter 14: Monitoring and Logging

Monitoring and logging are essential practices for ensuring that your LangFlow applications run smoothly and remain stable over time. With proper monitoring solutions in place, you can track the performance of your workflows, detect issues early, and troubleshoot efficiently. Logs provide valuable insights into application behavior and are crucial for debugging and analyzing production issues. In this chapter, we will cover how to implement effective monitoring solutions, adopt logging best practices, analyze logs for troubleshooting, create real-time monitoring dashboards, and set up alerts for incident management.

14.1. Implementing Monitoring Solutions

Monitoring is the process of tracking the performance and health of your LangFlow applications. By collecting data about system performance, you can detect potential issues before they escalate, optimize resources, and ensure that the system is operating as expected.

Several tools and services can be used to monitor LangFlow applications. These tools collect metrics, track performance, and provide valuable insights into system health.

- **Prometheus**: An open-source monitoring system that collects time-series data, such as CPU usage, memory consumption, and request latency. Prometheus is often used with **Grafana** to create custom dashboards.
- **Grafana**: A tool that integrates with Prometheus to visualize metrics and create real-time dashboards. It is ideal for tracking LangFlow application performance.
- **AWS CloudWatch**: A monitoring service for applications running on AWS. It collects logs, metrics, and events from EC2 instances, databases, and other AWS resources.
- **Google Cloud Monitoring**: Similar to AWS CloudWatch, this service provides monitoring for applications running on

Google Cloud Platform, offering tools to monitor performance and alert on failures.

- **Datadog**: A cloud-based monitoring platform that integrates with LangFlow to track metrics, logs, and events across distributed systems.

Example: Setting Up Prometheus to Monitor LangFlow

To set up Prometheus to monitor LangFlow, you need to instrument your application with Prometheus client libraries and expose a metrics endpoint. Here's an example using Python:

Install Prometheus Client for Python:
bash

```bash
pip install prometheus_client
```

Instrument LangFlow with Prometheus Metrics:
python

```python
from prometheus_client import start_http_server, Gauge

from langflow import LangFlowAgent


# Define a custom metric

workflow_duration = Gauge('langflow_workflow_duration_seconds', 'Time taken for LangFlow workflow to complete')


agent = LangFlowAgent(name="MetricsAgent")
```

138

```python
@agent.workflow

def example_workflow():

    import time

    start_time = time.time()

    # Simulate some processing

    time.sleep(2)

    # Update metric with workflow duration

    workflow_duration.set(time.time() - start_time)

    return "Workflow completed"


if __name__ == "__main__":

    # Start Prometheus server

    start_http_server(8000)

    agent.example_workflow()
```

1. *Explanation*: This example sets up a basic Prometheus server that exposes a custom metric (langflow_workflow_duration_seconds). The example_workflow function tracks the duration of a workflow and updates the metric accordingly. Prometheus can scrape this data at regular intervals to monitor workflow performance.

A monitoring dashboard helps visualize the metrics collected from your application, making it easier to track performance and detect issues. **Grafana** is a popular tool for creating real-time monitoring dashboards, which can pull data from Prometheus or other monitoring systems.

Steps to Create a Dashboard in Grafana:

1. **Install Grafana**: Follow the instructions at Grafana Downloads to install the platform.
2. **Configure Data Source**: In the Grafana UI, configure Prometheus or any other data source that collects LangFlow metrics.
3. **Create a Dashboard**:
   - Click on the "+" icon on the left sidebar and select "Dashboard."
   - Add panels to display metrics such as workflow durations, memory usage, or CPU load.
4. **Customize Dashboards**: Customize the appearance, set thresholds, and choose visualizations (graphs, tables, or heatmaps) that provide the most useful information.

Explanation: Grafana's flexibility allows you to create highly customized dashboards for monitoring LangFlow performance in real-time. You can visualize metrics like processing time, resource usage, and throughput to gain insights into system health.

14.2. Logging Best Practices

Logging is the process of recording application activity, providing a trail of events that can be reviewed for debugging, auditing, and performance analysis. Proper logging practices ensure that you have all the information you need to troubleshoot issues effectively.

Structured logging refers to the practice of logging data in a consistent, machine-readable format such as JSON. This makes it easier to parse logs and search for specific events.

Example of Structured Logging:

python

```python
import logging
import json

# Define the logger
logger = logging.getLogger('langflow')
logger.setLevel(logging.INFO)

# Create a log handler
handler = logging.StreamHandler()

# Define a log format
formatter = logging.Formatter('%(asctime)s - %(message)s')
handler.setFormatter(formatter)

# Add handler to logger
logger.addHandler(handler)

# Structured log example
log_data = {
    'event': 'workflow_started',
    'workflow_name': 'example_workflow',
```

```python
    'status': 'started',

    'user_id': 123

}


logger.info(json.dumps(log_data))
```

Explanation: This example demonstrates how to log events in a structured format using JSON. The json.dumps()method converts the log data into a JSON string, making it easier to parse and analyze. Structured logs are particularly useful when you need to aggregate logs across distributed systems.

Effective log management is crucial for handling large volumes of log data, especially in production environments. Here are some strategies:

- **Centralized Logging**: Use centralized logging services like **ELK Stack (Elasticsearch, Logstash, Kibana)** or **Splunk** to aggregate logs from multiple sources into a single location.
- **Log Rotation**: Implement log rotation to manage disk space and prevent logs from growing too large. Tools like **Logrotate** (on Linux systems) can automate this process.
- **Log Levels**: Use appropriate log levels (e.g., DEBUG, INFO, WARNING, ERROR) to filter logs based on severity. Avoid logging sensitive information at high verbosity levels.

14.3. Analyzing Logs for Troubleshooting

Logs provide valuable insights into your application's behavior and can help identify and resolve issues. By effectively analyzing logs, you can quickly pinpoint the cause of failures, performance bottlenecks, or other system issues.

There are several techniques for analyzing logs:

- **Search and Filter**: Use search queries to filter logs based on keywords, log levels, or specific events. This is useful when trying to locate specific issues (e.g., "error", "timeout").
- **Log Aggregation**: Combine logs from multiple services or applications to get a holistic view of the system. Tools like **ELK Stack** or **Splunk** provide powerful querying capabilities to search across large datasets.
- **Pattern Recognition**: Look for recurring patterns in the logs, such as repeated errors or slow response times. This can help identify root causes or areas for optimization.

Common issues that can be identified through log analysis include:

- **Application Failures**: Logs often contain stack traces or error messages that point to specific problems in the code.
- **Performance Issues**: Long-running operations or frequent timeouts can be identified through logs, allowing you to optimize workflows.
- **Resource Exhaustion**: Logs can indicate high memory or CPU usage, helping you pinpoint resource bottlenecks.

By combining log analysis with monitoring data, you can correlate performance issues with specific events or workflows, making troubleshooting more effective.

14.4. Real-Time Monitoring Dashboards

Real-time monitoring is crucial for tracking the performance of LangFlow applications while they are running. Dashboards display key metrics in real-time, allowing you to quickly detect problems and take corrective action.

Creating custom real-time dashboards allows you to visualize metrics that are relevant to your specific LangFlow application. Dashboards can display a variety of information, such as:

- **Workflow execution times**
- **System resource usage (CPU, memory)**
- **Error rates**
- **Throughput (requests per second)**

Example of Creating a Custom Dashboard in Grafana:

1. **Add a new panel**: In Grafana, click on "Add Panel" to create a new visualization.
2. **Select a data source**: Choose the data source (e.g., Prometheus or Elasticsearch).
3. **Create a query**: Write a query to fetch metrics related to LangFlow workflows (e.g., workflow_duration_seconds).
4. **Customize the visualization**: Choose a graph, bar chart, or table visualization based on the type of data you're displaying.

Some of the key metrics that are often visualized on real-time dashboards include:

- **Latency**: The time taken for a workflow to execute, which is important for real-time applications.
- **Error Rate**: The percentage of requests that result in errors, which can indicate problems with your workflows or external services.
- **Resource Usage**: Metrics such as CPU and memory usage can help identify performance bottlenecks and inefficient workflows.

14.5. Alerting and Incident Management

Alerting and incident management help you respond quickly to issues that arise in your LangFlow application. Alerts notify you when something goes wrong, and incident management helps you track and resolve those issues.

To set up alerts in monitoring systems like **Prometheus** or **CloudWatch**, define thresholds for key metrics, and configure notifications when those thresholds are exceeded.

Example of Setting Up an Alert in Prometheus:

yaml

```
groups:
- name: langflow-alerts
  rules:
  - alert: HighLatency
    expr: workflow_duration_seconds > 2
    for: 1m
    labels:
      severity: critical
    annotations:
      description: "Workflow execution took longer than expected."
      summary: "Workflow execution time exceeded threshold."
```

Explanation: This alert rule triggers if the workflow_duration_seconds metric exceeds 2 seconds for more than

1 minute. When the threshold is breached, Prometheus will notify you of the high latency.

Incident management involves tracking issues from detection to resolution:

- **Incident Tracking Tools**: Use tools like **JIRA**, **PagerDuty**, or **Opsgenie** to manage and track incidents.
- **Incident Response Plans**: Have a clear incident response plan in place, including predefined actions for various types of incidents (e.g., high CPU usage, workflow failures).
- **Post-Incident Review**: After resolving an incident, conduct a post-mortem review to identify the root cause and prevent future occurrences.

This chapter has covered the essential practices for monitoring and logging in LangFlow applications. From setting up monitoring solutions and dashboards to adopting logging best practices and implementing real-time alerting, these strategies help you maintain a healthy, high-performance system. By monitoring your LangFlow applications effectively and leveraging logs for troubleshooting, you can quickly identify and resolve issues, ensuring that your workflows continue to run smoothly.

Chapter 15: Extending LangFlow

LangFlow is a flexible and powerful platform that allows for customization, extension, and enhancement. As you build more complex workflows and AI agents, you may find the need to extend LangFlow's functionality to suit your specific use cases. This chapter will explore how you can extend LangFlow through developing plugins and extensions, contributing to the open-source community, leveraging third-party extensions, and designing custom integrations and middleware. Additionally, we will look at how to future-proof your LangFlow projects to ensure they remain adaptable and maintainable in the long term.

15.1. Developing Plugins and Extensions

One of LangFlow's greatest strengths is its extensibility. By developing plugins and extensions, you can tailor LangFlow to better meet your needs. Whether you're adding new features or enhancing existing ones, creating plugins is an excellent way to extend the platform.

LangFlow supports plugin development by providing a clear plugin architecture that is modular and easy to extend. Plugins can be added to LangFlow to enhance its functionality in specific areas like data processing, external API integrations, or custom workflows.

The basic structure of a LangFlow plugin typically includes:

- **Core Plugin File**: This contains the main logic of the plugin. It may define new nodes, workflows, or utilities.
- **Configuration**: Many plugins require configuration files to define their behavior. These may include environment settings, API keys, or workflow options.
- **Dependencies**: Plugins may depend on external libraries, which should be properly listed and installed.

Example of a Simple LangFlow Plugin:

python

```python
from langflow import LangFlowAgent, Node

# Define a custom node for a plugin
class MultiplyNode(Node):
    def process(self, input_data):
        if isinstance(input_data, (int, float)):
            return input_data * 2
        else:
            raise ValueError("Input must be an integer or float")

# Define the plugin
class MultiplyPlugin:
    def __init__(self):
        self.agent = LangFlowAgent(name="MultiplyPluginAgent")
        self.agent.add_node(MultiplyNode)

    def activate_plugin(self):
        return self.agent

plugin = MultiplyPlugin()
```

```
plugin.activate_plugin()
```

Explanation: In this simple example, a MultiplyPlugin is created, which adds a custom MultiplyNode to a LangFlow agent. The node multiplies input data by 2, and the plugin provides the functionality as an additional feature to the LangFlow application.

Once a plugin has been developed, it needs to be packaged and deployed. Here are the general steps for creating and deploying a LangFlow extension:

1. **Package the Plugin**: Create a package for your plugin, including any necessary dependencies, configuration files, and documentation.
2. **Testing**: Ensure that the plugin works as expected by running tests in your development environment.
3. **Deployment**: Deploy the plugin to the desired environment, either locally or to a production server. You may also distribute your plugin through a repository or package manager for other users to install.

To deploy a LangFlow extension, you can integrate it into your LangFlow application by importing the plugin and activating it as shown in the previous example.

15.2. Contributing to the LangFlow Open Source Community

LangFlow is an open-source platform, meaning anyone can contribute to its growth. Whether you're fixing bugs, adding features, or improving documentation, contributing to the open-source community helps the platform evolve and ensures its long-term success.

Open-source contribution involves making improvements to a project that is freely available for use, modification, and distribution. Contributing to LangFlow can include:

- **Fixing Bugs**: If you find an issue in LangFlow, submit a bug fix.
- **Adding Features**: Enhance LangFlow by adding new features or workflows.
- **Improving Documentation**: Clear, up-to-date documentation helps others understand how to use LangFlow.
- **Testing and Reviewing Code**: Test new features and review pull requests to ensure they meet the project's standards.

When contributing to LangFlow, it's essential to follow the guidelines set by the project maintainers. You should also test your changes thoroughly before submitting a pull request.

Collaboration in open-source projects requires clear communication and adherence to community guidelines. Here are some best practices:

- **Fork the Repository**: Always fork the LangFlow repository before making changes. This ensures that you have your own copy of the project.
- **Work in Branches**: Create separate branches for each feature or bug fix you work on. This helps keep your code organized and avoids conflicts.
- **Write Tests**: Always write tests for your changes. This helps maintain the quality and stability of the project.
- **Follow Coding Standards**: Stick to the coding conventions and formatting rules set by the LangFlow project.

Example of Contributing Code:

bash

```
# Fork the repository and clone it to your local machine
```

```
git clone https://github.com/your-username/langflow.git

cd langflow


# Create a new branch for your feature or fix

git checkout -b new-feature


# Make your changes, commit them, and push them to your
fork

git add .

git commit -m "Added new feature"

git push origin new-feature


# Open a pull request on GitHub to merge your changes
```

15.3. Leveraging Third-Party Extensions

In addition to developing your own plugins, LangFlow supports third-party extensions that can be integrated into your workflows. These extensions can add significant functionality, from connecting to external services to enhancing your system with machine learning models.

LangFlow's open-source ecosystem encourages the development of community plugins, which can be easily integrated into your workflows. These plugins extend LangFlow's capabilities by providing ready-made solutions for common tasks, such as data visualization, authentication, and integration with cloud platforms.

To integrate a third-party plugin, follow these steps:

1. **Find the Plugin**: Search for the plugin in repositories, such as GitHub or LangFlow's official plugin store (if available).
2. **Install the Plugin**: Install the plugin using pip or another package manager, depending on how the plugin is distributed.
3. **Configure the Plugin**: Set up any necessary configuration files, such as API keys or environment variables.
4. **Integrate into Your Workflow**: Import the plugin into your LangFlow application and use it within your workflows.

Example of Installing and Using a Third-Party Plugin:

bash

```
# Install the plugin using pip

pip install langflow-plugin-example


# Use the plugin in your LangFlow workflow

from langflow_plugin_example import ExamplePlugin


agent = LangFlowAgent(name="ThirdPartyAgent")

plugin = ExamplePlugin()

agent.add_plugin(plugin)
```

Explanation: This example shows how to install a third-party LangFlow plugin and integrate it into an agent's workflow.

When evaluating third-party extensions, consider the following criteria:

- **Compatibility**: Ensure the plugin or extension is compatible with your version of LangFlow.
- **Documentation**: Well-documented plugins are easier to integrate and use.
- **Community Support**: A strong community behind a plugin can provide valuable assistance and ensure that the plugin is actively maintained.
- **Security**: Make sure that the third-party plugin adheres to best security practices, especially if it handles sensitive data.

15.4. Custom Integrations and Middleware

Custom integrations and middleware solutions can enhance LangFlow by connecting it to other applications or systems, allowing it to perform complex tasks or interact with external services.

Middleware is software that acts as an intermediary between two systems or components. In LangFlow, middleware can be used to handle tasks such as logging, authentication, or caching within workflows.

To design middleware for LangFlow:

1. **Identify Interactions**: Determine which parts of your workflow require external integration or additional processing.
2. **Write the Middleware**: Create functions or classes that process data before it reaches the main workflow or after it has been processed.

3. **Integrate with LangFlow**: Add your middleware to the workflow pipeline, ensuring that it's called at the appropriate stage.

Example of Custom Middleware:

python

```python
from langflow import LangFlowAgent


class AuthMiddleware:
    def __init__(self, agent):
        self.agent = agent

    def before_processing(self, input_data):
        if "auth_token" not in input_data:
            raise ValueError("Authentication token is missing")
        return input_data


# Define the agent with middleware
agent = LangFlowAgent(name="AuthMiddlewareAgent")
middleware = AuthMiddleware(agent)
agent.add_middleware(middleware.before_processing)
```

```python
@agent.workflow
def process_data(input_data):

    return f"Processed data: {input_data}"


# Example usage

input_data = {"auth_token": "abc123", "data":
"important_data"}

result = agent.process_data(input_data)

print(result)
```

Explanation: This middleware checks for the presence of an authentication token before processing data. If the token is missing, it raises an error; otherwise, it allows the data to proceed to the workflow.

Custom integrations allow LangFlow to work seamlessly with other services and tools. Whether integrating with databases, third-party APIs, or cloud platforms, these integrations enhance the flexibility of LangFlow workflows.

Example of a Custom API Integration:

python

```python
import requests


class CustomAPIIntegration:
```

```python
def fetch_data(self, api_url):

    response = requests.get(api_url)

    if response.status_code == 200:

        return response.json()

    else:

        return {"error": "Failed to fetch data"}


api_integration = CustomAPIIntegration()

data = api_integration.fetch_data("https://api.example.com/data")

print(data)
```

Explanation: This example demonstrates how to integrate a custom API within LangFlow. The CustomAPIIntegration class fetches data from an external API and returns the response as JSON.

15.5. Future-Proofing Your LangFlow Projects

As technology evolves, it's important to ensure that your LangFlow projects remain adaptable to future changes. Future-proofing your projects helps ensure that they can scale with new technologies, tools, and user needs.

To adapt to technological changes:

- **Stay Updated**: Regularly update your LangFlow application to benefit from the latest features, security patches, and optimizations.
- **Modular Architecture**: Design your workflows and agents with modularity in mind, making it easier to replace or upgrade components without affecting the entire system.
- **Cloud-Native Solutions**: Leverage cloud-native tools and services to ensure that your LangFlow application can scale efficiently as your needs grow.

For long-term maintainability:

- **Write Clean, Maintainable Code**: Use consistent coding standards, modularize your workflows, and include ample documentation to make the codebase easy to manage.
- **Automate Testing**: Implement automated testing to ensure that updates don't break existing functionality.
- **Monitor System Health**: Continuously monitor the system to detect and resolve issues before they become critical.

This chapter has explored the various ways you can extend LangFlow, from developing custom plugins and extensions to contributing to the open-source community, leveraging third-party tools, and creating custom integrations. By adopting best practices for extending LangFlow and future-proofing your projects, you can ensure that your LangFlow applications remain flexible, scalable, and maintainable in the years to come.

Chapter 16: Real-World Applications and Case Studies

LangFlow's flexibility and scalability make it a powerful tool for solving real-world challenges across various industries. In this chapter, we will explore a variety of use cases where LangFlow has been effectively applied. These examples will cover enterprise automation, AI-powered customer support, data analytics, IoT integrations, and specialized applications in healthcare and fintech. By understanding these real-world applications, you can gain insights into how to adapt LangFlow to your specific needs.

16.1. Enterprise Automation with LangFlow

LangFlow can automate and streamline business processes, making it an ideal tool for enterprise applications. Automation in enterprises improves efficiency, reduces human error, and accelerates workflows.

In large organizations, manual tasks such as data entry, customer interactions, and inventory management can be time-consuming and prone to error. LangFlow can automate these processes by building workflows that handle repetitive tasks efficiently.

Example: Automating Invoice Processing

A company receives invoices from various vendors, and these invoices need to be processed and stored in a database. LangFlow can automate this process by building a workflow that:

1. Extracts data from invoices using Optical Character Recognition (OCR).
2. Validates the extracted data (e.g., checking for missing information or incorrect formats).
3. Stores the validated data in a database or accounting software.

python

```python
from langflow import LangFlowAgent, Node
import pytesseract
from PIL import Image


class OCRNode(Node):
    def process(self, image_path):
        img = Image.open(image_path)
        text = pytesseract.image_to_string(img)
        return text


class ValidationNode(Node):
    def process(self, invoice_data):
        # Validate invoice format
        if "total" in invoice_data and "vendor_name" in invoice_data:
            return True
        return False


agent = LangFlowAgent(name="InvoiceProcessingAgent")
ocr_node = OCRNode()
validation_node = ValidationNode()
```

```
agent.add_node(ocr_node)

agent.add_node(validation_node)


@agent.workflow

def process_invoice(image_path):

    invoice_data = ocr_node.process(image_path)

    is_valid = validation_node.process(invoice_data)

    if is_valid:

        # Store in database

        return "Invoice Processed Successfully"

    else:

        return "Invalid Invoice Data"
```

Explanation: This example uses LangFlow to automate invoice processing. The OCRNode extracts text from an image using OCR, and the ValidationNode checks if the necessary data exists in the extracted text. If the data is valid, it can be processed further (e.g., stored in a database).

LangFlow also supports integration with various enterprise systems, such as **ERP (Enterprise Resource Planning)**, **CRM (Customer Relationship Management)**, and **HR systems**. By integrating these systems, businesses can automate workflows across departments and systems.

For instance, LangFlow can integrate with a CRM system to automatically log customer interactions, create follow-up tasks, and update customer records based on workflow outcomes.

16.2. AI-Powered Customer Support Agents

AI-powered chatbots and customer support agents are transforming how businesses interact with customers. LangFlow can be used to build intelligent AI agents that enhance the customer experience and automate support tasks.

LangFlow can help design chatbots that understand natural language, respond intelligently to user inquiries, and integrate with various backend systems to provide real-time solutions. These chatbots can handle tasks such as answering frequently asked questions (FAQs), processing orders, and routing complex issues to human agents.

Example: Building a Customer Support Chatbot:

python

```python
from langflow import LangFlowAgent, Node

from transformers import pipeline


class NLPNode(Node):

    def process(self, text):

        # Use a pre-trained model for language understanding

        nlp = pipeline("question-answering")
```

```python
    result = nlp(question="What is the order status?",
context=text)

    return result['answer']


agent = LangFlowAgent(name="SupportAgent")

nlp_node = NLPNode()


agent.add_node(nlp_node)


@agent.workflow

def handle_customer_query(customer_text):

  response = nlp_node.process(customer_text)

  return response
```

Explanation: This example uses LangFlow to build a chatbot that answers customer queries based on a given text (e.g., order details). The NLPNode uses a pre-trained transformer model to understand customer inquiries and provide answers accordingly.

AI-powered support agents provide several benefits for customers:

- **24/7 Availability**: Customers can interact with support agents at any time.
- **Personalization**: AI agents can provide personalized responses based on customer data and previous interactions.
- **Efficiency**: AI agents can handle a high volume of queries simultaneously, reducing waiting times for customers.

16.3. Data Analytics and Business Intelligence

LangFlow can be leveraged to build data pipelines and enhance business intelligence (BI) systems by processing and analyzing data for decision-making. It can integrate with data sources, clean and transform data, and generate insights that drive business strategies.

LangFlow workflows can automate data ingestion, transformation, and storage. For example, a company might want to analyze sales data across multiple regions, cleanse it, and generate reports for management.

Example: Building a Simple Data Pipeline:

python

```python
import pandas as pd

from langflow import LangFlowAgent, Node


class DataIngestionNode(Node):
    def process(self, data_source):
        # Load data from a CSV file
        return pd.read_csv(data_source)


class DataCleaningNode(Node):
    def process(self, data):
        # Remove rows with missing values
```

```python
    return data.dropna()


agent = LangFlowAgent(name="DataPipelineAgent")

ingestion_node = DataIngestionNode()

cleaning_node = DataCleaningNode()


agent.add_node(ingestion_node)

agent.add_node(cleaning_node)


@agent.workflow

def process_sales_data(data_source):

    raw_data = ingestion_node.process(data_source)

    clean_data = cleaning_node.process(raw_data)

    return clean_data.describe()  # Generate summary statistics
```

Explanation: This workflow defines a simple data pipeline where DataIngestionNode ingests data from a CSV file, and DataCleaningNode cleans the data by removing rows with missing values. The output is summary statistics of the cleaned data.

After processing the data, LangFlow can integrate with BI tools like **Tableau**, **Power BI**, or even Python libraries like **Matplotlib** and **Plotly** to generate visualizations of the data. These insights help stakeholders make informed decisions.

16.4. IoT Integrations and Smart Workflows

LangFlow's versatility extends to integrating with the Internet of Things (IoT), enabling the creation of smart workflows that process data from IoT devices in real-time.

LangFlow can connect to IoT devices, collect sensor data, and trigger workflows based on specific conditions. For example, you could integrate LangFlow with an IoT temperature sensor to automate actions when temperature thresholds are crossed.

Example: Integrating with an IoT Temperature Sensor:

python

```python
import random

from langflow import LangFlowAgent, Node


class TemperatureSensorNode(Node):
    def process(self):
        # Simulate temperature sensor reading
        return random.uniform(20, 30)  # Temperature in Celsius


class AlertNode(Node):
    def process(self, temperature):
        if temperature > 25:
```

```python
        return "High Temperature Alert!"

    return "Temperature is normal."


agent = LangFlowAgent(name="IoTTemperatureAgent")

sensor_node = TemperatureSensorNode()

alert_node = AlertNode()


agent.add_node(sensor_node)

agent.add_node(alert_node)


@agent.workflow

def monitor_temperature():

    temperature = sensor_node.process()

    alert = alert_node.process(temperature)

    return alert
```

Explanation: This example simulates an IoT temperature sensor that generates random temperature values. The AlertNode triggers an alert if the temperature exceeds 25°C. LangFlow's workflow can be adapted to real-time data from physical devices.

LangFlow can also process real-time data streams from IoT devices, providing immediate feedback and enabling timely decision-making. Real-time processing can be achieved by using frameworks like **Apache Kafka** or **AWS Kinesis** to manage data streams.

16.5. Healthcare and Fintech Applications

LangFlow has potential applications in industries that require high security, compliance, and real-time processing. Two such industries are healthcare and fintech.

In healthcare and fintech, data security, privacy, and compliance with regulations like **HIPAA** (Health Insurance Portability and Accountability Act) and **PCI-DSS** (Payment Card Industry Data Security Standard) are paramount. LangFlow workflows that handle sensitive data must incorporate encryption, access control, and audit logging.

Example: Securing Healthcare Data Workflow:

python

```python
from cryptography.fernet import Fernet


class SecureDataNode(Node):
    def __init__(self, key):
        self.cipher_suite = Fernet(key)


    def process(self, sensitive_data):
        encrypted_data = self.cipher_suite.encrypt(sensitive_data.encode())
        return encrypted_data
```

```
# Generate a key for encryption

key = Fernet.generate_key()

secure_node = SecureDataNode(key)


# Encrypt patient data

patient_data = "Patient Name: John Doe, SSN: 123-45-6789"

encrypted_data = secure_node.process(patient_data)

print(encrypted_data)
```

Explanation: This example demonstrates how to secure sensitive healthcare data using encryption in LangFlow. The SecureDataNode class encrypts the patient data to ensure it remains private and protected.

In healthcare, LangFlow can automate medical record processing, diagnostic support, and patient monitoring. In fintech, it can be used for fraud detection, automated trading, and risk assessment.

For example, LangFlow could be used to automate the process of analyzing credit card transactions and identifying potentially fraudulent activities based on pre-defined patterns or machine learning models.

This chapter has explored a wide range of real-world applications of LangFlow, including enterprise automation, AI-powered customer support, data analytics, IoT integrations, and specialized applications in healthcare and fintech. LangFlow's versatility enables it to be used across industries for automating tasks, integrating systems, and creating intelligent workflows. By leveraging LangFlow, businesses and organizations can improve efficiency, enhance customer experience, and drive data-driven decision-making.

Chapter 17: Troubleshooting Common Issues

Troubleshooting is an essential skill when working with LangFlow, as it ensures that your workflows run smoothly and reliably. In this chapter, we will explore common issues you might encounter while working with LangFlow applications, covering debugging techniques, integration failures, performance bottlenecks, security vulnerabilities, and how to make use of community resources for troubleshooting.

17.1. Debugging LangFlow Workflows

When building workflows in LangFlow, errors are inevitable. Debugging is the process of identifying and resolving these issues to ensure the system behaves as expected. LangFlow provides several tools and strategies for efficient debugging.

Common errors in LangFlow workflows typically arise from issues such as:

- **Input Validation Errors**: Often, workflows fail when input data doesn't meet the expected format or type.
- **Node Execution Failures**: If a node in the workflow is misconfigured or encounters an error, the entire workflow might fail.
- **Timeouts**: Long-running tasks or external service calls can lead to timeouts if not handled correctly.
- **Data Mismatches**: When data passed between nodes doesn't align with the expected structure, errors can occur.

To effectively identify errors, monitor logs, review error messages, and inspect workflow outputs at each node.

Example: Common Error in a Workflow:

python

```python
from langflow import LangFlowAgent, Node


class ExampleNode(Node):
    def process(self, input_data):
        if not isinstance(input_data, int):
            raise ValueError("Expected an integer input")
        return input_data * 2


agent = LangFlowAgent(name="ExampleAgent")
node = ExampleNode()
agent.add_node(node)


@agent.workflow
def example_workflow(input_data):
    result = node.process(input_data)
    return result


# Simulate passing an invalid input type
try:
    example_workflow("invalid_input")
except Exception as e:
```

```python
print(f"Error: {e}")
```

Explanation: In this example, the ExampleNode raises an error when it receives a string instead of an integer. This is a typical input validation error, and the exception handling ensures that the error is captured and displayed.

Effective debugging involves several approaches:

Print Statements: Use print() or logging statements at key points in the workflow to inspect data at various stages.
Example:
python

```python
print(f"Received input: {input_data}")
```

Use Debugging Tools: Leverage Python's built-in debugger (pdb) to step through your code interactively and inspect variables at runtime.
Example:
python

```python
import pdb

pdb.set_trace()
```

- **Workflow Inspection**: LangFlow provides an interface to inspect each node's inputs and outputs. Reviewing these can help you identify where things go wrong.

17.2. Resolving Integration Failures

LangFlow often integrates with external APIs, services, and databases. Integration failures can occur when there are issues with connecting to these services or when the data format doesn't match expectations.

When working with APIs, common issues include:

- **Authentication Failures**: Ensure that API keys, tokens, or credentials are correct and properly configured.
- **API Rate Limiting**: Some APIs limit the number of requests that can be made in a given period. Handle rate limits with retries or backoff strategies.
- **Timeouts**: External APIs may take too long to respond, resulting in timeouts.

Example: Handling API Connection Failure:

python

```python
import requests

from requests.exceptions import RequestException


def fetch_data_from_api(api_url):
    try:

        response = requests.get(api_url, timeout=5)  # Set a timeout for the request

        response.raise_for_status()  # Raise an error for bad status codes

        return response.json()
```

```
    except RequestException as e:

        print(f"Error fetching data: {e}")

        return None


data =
fetch_data_from_api("https://api.example.com/data")
```

Explanation: This example demonstrates how to handle API connection failures, including timeouts and invalid responses. The requests.exceptions.RequestException captures any errors that occur during the API call.

If a service you're integrating with is down, workflows may fail due to unavailable resources. To handle service downtimes:

- **Retry Mechanisms**: Implement retry mechanisms with exponential backoff to handle intermittent failures.
- **Graceful Error Handling**: Instead of crashing the workflow, log the error and return a fallback value or message.

17.3. Handling Performance Bottlenecks

As LangFlow applications scale, performance bottlenecks can arise. Identifying and addressing these issues ensures that workflows run efficiently and within acceptable time limits.

Performance issues can arise from:

- **Heavy Computation**: Long-running calculations or data processing tasks can slow down workflows.
- **External Dependencies**: Latency from external APIs or databases can introduce delays.

- **Inefficient Data Structures**: Using inefficient data structures or algorithms can negatively impact performance.

Example: Identifying a Performance Bottleneck:

python

```python
import time

def slow_function():
    time.sleep(2)  # Simulate a delay

start_time = time.time()
slow_function()
print(f"Function took {time.time() - start_time} seconds")
```

Explanation: This code simulates a performance bottleneck where a function takes a long time to execute. By measuring the execution time, you can identify areas that need optimization.

To optimize performance:

- **Use Caching**: Cache frequently accessed data to reduce redundant processing.
- **Parallelism**: Break down tasks into smaller, parallelizable chunks to speed up computation.
- **Optimize Data Access**: Use efficient queries when interacting with databases to avoid long response times.

17.4. Addressing Security Vulnerabilities

LangFlow applications often interact with sensitive data, making security a top priority. Identifying and mitigating security vulnerabilities ensures the integrity and privacy of your application.

Common security issues include:

- **Injection Attacks**: Where malicious input is executed as part of a query, causing unintended actions.
- **Cross-Site Scripting (XSS)**: Where malicious scripts are injected into web applications, potentially compromising user data.
- **Insecure Data Storage**: Storing sensitive data (such as passwords or API keys) in an insecure manner.

Example: Preventing SQL Injection:

python

```python
import mysql.connector


def fetch_user_data(user_id):

    connection = mysql.connector.connect(host='localhost', user='user', password='pass', database='users_db')

    cursor = connection.cursor()

    cursor.execute("SELECT * FROM users WHERE id = %s", (user_id,))  # Parameterized query

    return cursor.fetchall()
```

Explanation: This example demonstrates how to protect against SQL injection by using parameterized queries. The %splaceholder ensures that user input is properly sanitized before being used in the SQL query.

To mitigate security risks:

- **Input Validation**: Always validate and sanitize user inputs to avoid injection attacks.
- **Encryption**: Use encryption for sensitive data, both at rest and in transit.
- **Use Secure Libraries**: Ensure that third-party libraries and dependencies are secure and up to date.

17.5. Community Resources for Troubleshooting

The LangFlow community offers a wealth of resources to help troubleshoot common issues. Engaging with the community can provide valuable insights, solutions, and assistance from other developers.

LangFlow has an active community that can provide support for troubleshooting:

- **Stack Overflow**: A great place to ask questions and find solutions to common LangFlow-related issues.
- **LangFlow GitHub Discussions**: Participate in discussions about bugs, features, and troubleshooting.
- **Reddit**: Some subreddits, such as r/MachineLearning, often discuss tools like LangFlow and related topics.

Engaging with these communities allows you to leverage the knowledge of other developers who may have faced similar issues.

LangFlow's official documentation is a critical resource for troubleshooting. It provides detailed information about the platform's features, common errors, and configuration options. Always consult the documentation when you encounter an issue, as it is often the quickest way to find a solution.

This chapter has covered essential troubleshooting techniques for common issues you may encounter while working with LangFlow. By identifying common errors, resolving integration failures, handling performance bottlenecks, addressing security vulnerabilities, and leveraging community resources, you can ensure that your LangFlow applications remain robust and functional. Troubleshooting is an ongoing process, but with the right tools and strategies, you can resolve issues efficiently and keep your workflows running smoothly.

Chapter 18: Best Practices and Design Patterns

Building efficient and maintainable workflows in LangFlow requires a thoughtful approach to design. Adopting best practices and using design patterns helps ensure that workflows are modular, efficient, and easy to maintain. This chapter covers modular design principles, efficient workflow structuring, reusability, error-resilient workflow design, and best practices for documentation and code commenting. Following these guidelines will not only make your LangFlow projects more robust but also easier to scale and collaborate on.

18.1. Modular Design Principles

Modular design is the practice of breaking down a system into smaller, self-contained components, each responsible for a specific function. LangFlow's flexibility allows you to build modular workflows that are easier to maintain and extend. By adhering to modular design principles, you can enhance the scalability and readability of your workflows.

A modular workflow in LangFlow consists of individual nodes that perform specific tasks, such as data transformation, API calls, or business logic. Each node should have a single responsibility, making it easier to test, debug, and modify independently of other parts of the workflow.

Example: Building a Modular Workflow with LangFlow:

python

```
from langflow import LangFlowAgent, Node


class InputValidationNode(Node):
```

```python
    def process(self, input_data):

        if not isinstance(input_data, str):

            raise ValueError("Input must be a string")

        return input_data


class DataTransformationNode(Node):

    def process(self, input_data):

        return input_data.upper()


agent = LangFlowAgent(name="ModularAgent")

validation_node = InputValidationNode()

transformation_node = DataTransformationNode()


agent.add_node(validation_node)

agent.add_node(transformation_node)


@agent.workflow

def process_data(input_data):

    validated_data = validation_node.process(input_data)

    transformed_data = transformation_node.process(validated_data)

    return transformed_data
```

Explanation: This example demonstrates a modular workflow where each node performs a specific task. The InputValidationNode ensures that the input data is a string, while the DataTransformationNode converts the string to uppercase. By separating concerns into distinct nodes, we can easily modify, test, and scale each node independently.

Modular architecture offers several advantages:

- **Maintainability**: Smaller, independent modules are easier to understand and maintain.
- **Reusability**: Once a module is created, it can be reused across different workflows, reducing the need to rewrite code.
- **Scalability**: New functionality can be added by introducing new nodes without modifying existing ones.
- **Testability**: Individual modules can be tested in isolation, making it easier to identify and fix bugs.

18.2. Efficient Workflow Structuring

Structuring your LangFlow workflows efficiently is key to ensuring readability, scalability, and ease of maintenance. A well-organized workflow improves collaboration, especially when multiple developers work on the same project.

When organizing workflow components, ensure that each component has a clear, defined purpose. Components should be logically grouped based on their functionality. Additionally, workflows should be modular, with clear inputs and outputs for each node.

Best Practices for Organizing Workflow Components:

- **Group Similar Tasks**: Group nodes that perform similar operations together (e.g., data transformation, API calls).
- **Use Descriptive Names**: Name nodes and workflows descriptively to make it clear what each component does.

- **Limit Workflow Length**: Break down long workflows into smaller sub-workflows or pipelines to improve readability.

Readability is crucial for maintaining and understanding workflows. To improve readability:

- **Use Clear Naming Conventions**: Name workflows, nodes, and variables in a way that describes their purpose.
- **Comment Key Parts of the Workflow**: Write comments explaining the functionality of complex nodes or sections of the workflow.
- **Maintain Consistent Formatting**: Use consistent indentation and spacing to enhance the structure of the workflow.

Example: Readable Workflow:

python

```python
from langflow import LangFlowAgent, Node


# Input Validation Node
class InputValidationNode(Node):
    def process(self, input_data):
        # Ensure the input is a string
        if not isinstance(input_data, str):
            raise ValueError("Expected a string input")
        return input_data
```

```python
# Data Transformation Node
class DataTransformationNode(Node):
    def process(self, input_data):
        # Convert input string to uppercase
        return input_data.upper()


# Main Agent
agent = LangFlowAgent(name="ReadableAgent")
validation_node = InputValidationNode()
transformation_node = DataTransformationNode()


# Add nodes to the agent
agent.add_node(validation_node)
agent.add_node(transformation_node)


# Define workflow
@agent.workflow
def process_data(input_data):
    validated_data = validation_node.process(input_data)  # Validate input
```

```python
    transformed_data =
transformation_node.process(validated_data)  #
Transform data

    return transformed_data
```

Explanation: This example focuses on enhancing readability by clearly naming nodes and adding comments that explain their purpose. This makes the code easier to understand for other developers.

18.3. Reusability and DRY (Don't Repeat Yourself)

One of the key principles in software development is to avoid redundancy. The **DRY (Don't Repeat Yourself)** principle encourages developers to eliminate duplicate code and promote reusability across workflows.

Reusability is achieved by designing components that can be used in multiple workflows without modification. Nodes that are generic and decoupled from specific use cases are the easiest to reuse. For example, a node that processes input data by trimming whitespace can be used in various workflows.

Example: Reusable Node:

python

```python
class TrimWhitespaceNode(Node):

    def process(self, input_data):

        return input_data.strip()
```

Explanation: By creating a TrimWhitespaceNode, we can reuse this logic across multiple workflows without rewriting the same functionality.

Avoid redundant code by:

- **Creating Helper Functions**: For commonly repeated tasks, create helper functions or nodes.
- **Using Libraries**: Leverage existing libraries and frameworks that provide commonly used functionality.
- **Modularizing**: Break down large workflows into smaller, reusable sub-workflows.

18.4. Error-Resilient Workflow Design

Workflows must be designed to handle errors gracefully, especially when interacting with external systems or processing large datasets. Building fault tolerance into workflows ensures that errors are caught and handled appropriately, preventing crashes or unwanted side effects.

Fault tolerance means designing workflows so that they can continue functioning even when certain components fail. This can involve:

- **Error Handling**: Use try-except blocks to catch exceptions and handle them gracefully.
- **Retry Mechanisms**: For external service calls, implement retries in case of transient failures (e.g., network errors).

Example: Error Handling in Workflow:

python

```python
class RetryNode(Node):
    def process(self, input_data):
        retry_count = 3
        for _ in range(retry_count):
            try:
                # Simulate an external API call
                if input_data == "fail":
                    raise ValueError("Simulated error")
                return "Success"
            except Exception as e:
                print(f"Error: {e}, Retrying...")
        return "Failed after retries"


agent = LangFlowAgent(name="RetryAgent")
retry_node = RetryNode()
agent.add_node(retry_node)


@agent.workflow
def process_data(input_data):
```

```
return retry_node.process(input_data)
```

Explanation: This RetryNode attempts to process the input data and retries the operation up to 3 times in case of errors. The error is handled gracefully, and the workflow doesn't fail abruptly.

Retry mechanisms are essential for handling transient issues, such as network failures. When implementing retries, consider using **exponential backoff** to avoid overwhelming the system with frequent retries.

18.5. Documentation and Code Commenting Standards

Clear documentation and code comments are vital for ensuring that workflows are understandable and maintainable. Well-documented workflows and components also make it easier for new developers to contribute to the project.

Documentation should describe the purpose of each component, how it works, and how to use it. It should also explain the inputs and outputs of workflows and nodes.

Best Practices for Writing Documentation:

- **Describe the Purpose**: Clearly explain what each node or workflow does.
- **Provide Examples**: Include code examples or use cases that demonstrate how to use the workflow or component.
- **Document Inputs and Outputs**: Describe the expected inputs and outputs for each node or workflow.

Code comments should provide clarity about the functionality of the code, particularly for complex logic. The comments should be concise but descriptive enough to explain the reasoning behind certain decisions.

Best Practices for Code Commenting:

- **Explain Why, Not What**: Focus on explaining why certain decisions were made, rather than stating what the code does (which is often obvious).
- **Comment Complex Logic**: Write comments to explain any complex or non-obvious parts of the workflow.
- **Use Consistent Style**: Follow a consistent commenting style throughout the codebase.

Example of Good Commenting:

python

```python
# This node converts input data to uppercase

class UppercaseNode(Node):

    def process(self, input_data):

        # Ensure input is a string before processing

        if not isinstance(input_data, str):

            raise ValueError("Input must be a string")

        return input_data.upper()
```

Explanation: The comments explain both the purpose of the node and the reasoning behind the validation logic, providing clarity for future developers.

This chapter has provided insights into best practices and design patterns for LangFlow workflows. By following modular design principles, structuring workflows efficiently, and emphasizing reusability, you can create robust, scalable applications. Additionally, adopting error-resilient practices and adhering to documentation and commenting standards will ensure that your workflows remain maintainable and understandable over time.

Chapter 19: Future Trends and Innovations in LangFlow

LangFlow is a dynamic platform that continues to evolve, integrating new technologies and enhancing existing features to meet the demands of modern applications. In this chapter, we will explore some of the key future trends and innovations shaping LangFlow, including advancements in AI and machine learning, integration with emerging technologies like blockchain and AR/VR, automated workflow generation, edge computing, and predictions for LangFlow's future role in the AI landscape.

19.1. AI and Machine Learning Advancements

The world of artificial intelligence (AI) and machine learning (ML) is rapidly evolving, with new advancements happening regularly. LangFlow is well-positioned to take advantage of these advancements, enabling developers to integrate cutting-edge AI models and machine learning techniques into their workflows.

The field of AI is witnessing several emerging technologies that are poised to transform workflows and applications built with LangFlow. These include:

- **Generative AI**: Models such as GPT (Generative Pretrained Transformers) are becoming increasingly capable of generating human-like text, images, and even code. LangFlow can leverage these models to automate content creation, chatbots, and other intelligent systems.
- **Few-Shot Learning**: Few-shot learning algorithms can learn new tasks with a minimal amount of data. This will enable LangFlow to work with limited datasets, making it more efficient for applications where large amounts of labeled data are not available.
- **Reinforcement Learning**: Reinforcement learning (RL) focuses on teaching agents to make decisions by interacting with their environment. Integrating RL into LangFlow

workflows can lead to the development of intelligent agents capable of optimizing their actions in real-time.

- **Federated Learning**: This technology allows models to be trained across decentralized devices without sharing sensitive data, making it particularly useful for privacy-sensitive applications.

Example: Integrating GPT-3 into LangFlow:

python

```python
from langflow import LangFlowAgent, Node

import openai


openai.api_key = "your-openai-api-key"


class GPT3Node(Node):
    def process(self, input_data):
        response = openai.Completion.create(
            engine="text-davinci-003",
            prompt=input_data,
            max_tokens=150
        )
        return response.choices[0].text.strip()
```

```python
agent = LangFlowAgent(name="GPT3Agent")

gpt3_node = GPT3Node()


agent.add_node(gpt3_node)


@agent.workflow

def generate_text(input_data):

    return gpt3_node.process(input_data)
```

Explanation: This example shows how LangFlow can integrate with the GPT-3 API to generate text responses based on input data. LangFlow can leverage cutting-edge AI models to enhance workflows that require natural language processing capabilities.

As machine learning models continue to improve, LangFlow will benefit from the ability to integrate state-of-the-art models, such as deep neural networks (DNNs), convolutional neural networks (CNNs), and transformer-based models. These models can be used to improve tasks like image recognition, speech-to-text, and sentiment analysis.

LangFlow will provide developers with easy-to-use nodes and APIs to integrate these models directly into their workflows, allowing for more powerful and intelligent applications.

19.2. Integration with Emerging Technologies (Blockchain, AR/VR)

LangFlow's ability to integrate with emerging technologies opens up new possibilities for creating innovative workflows. As blockchain, augmented reality (AR), and virtual reality (VR) continue to gain traction, LangFlow can be used to automate processes and create smarter systems that leverage these technologies.

Blockchain technology, which is known for its decentralization, immutability, and security, can be integrated with LangFlow to build systems that require secure transactions and trustless environments. Use cases include:

- **Smart Contracts**: Automating contract execution with blockchain-based smart contracts.
- **Decentralized Finance (DeFi)**: LangFlow can help automate financial transactions, lending, and trading processes in the decentralized finance space.
- **Supply Chain Management**: Blockchain's transparency can be leveraged to automate and track products across the supply chain in a LangFlow workflow.

Example: Integrating Blockchain for Supply Chain Tracking:

python

```python
from langflow import LangFlowAgent, Node

from web3 import Web3


class BlockchainNode(Node):

    def __init__(self, contract_address, abi):
```

```python
        self.web3 =
Web3(Web3.HTTPProvider('https://mainnet.infura.io/v3/y
our-project-id'))

        self.contract =
self.web3.eth.contract(address=contract_address, abi=abi)


    def process(self, transaction_data):

        # Example: Calling a smart contract method to store
transaction data

        tx_hash =
self.contract.functions.storeTransaction(transaction_data).
transact()

        self.web3.eth.waitForTransactionReceipt(tx_hash)

        return f"Transaction stored: {tx_hash}"


# Smart contract ABI and address (mock example)

contract_address = "0xYourSmartContractAddress"

contract_abi = [...]  # Smart contract ABI


agent = LangFlowAgent(name="BlockchainAgent")

blockchain_node = BlockchainNode(contract_address,
contract_abi)


agent.add_node(blockchain_node)
```

```
@agent.workflow

def track_transaction(transaction_data):

  return blockchain_node.process(transaction_data)
```

Explanation: This example demonstrates how LangFlow can integrate with a blockchain to track transactions using a smart contract. LangFlow can automate interactions with the blockchain, storing transaction data securely.

Augmented reality (AR) and virtual reality (VR) technologies are rapidly advancing, and LangFlow can integrate with AR/VR systems to create immersive experiences. Use cases for AR/VR in LangFlow workflows include:

- **Training Simulations**: LangFlow can automate training simulations for industries like healthcare or manufacturing, providing interactive, immersive learning experiences.
- **Product Visualization**: LangFlow can power workflows that generate AR-based product visualizations, allowing customers to see products in real-time using their smartphones or VR headsets.

19.3. Automated Workflow Generation

One of the most exciting future trends for LangFlow is the integration of AI-driven tools that automatically generate workflows. These tools will simplify the workflow creation process, allowing developers to focus on high-level logic and leave the automation to the system.

AI-driven workflow generation will enable LangFlow to automatically create workflows based on specific business requirements or natural language descriptions. These tools will use machine learning models to understand user intentions and generate corresponding workflows.

For example, an AI system could be trained to automatically create a workflow for processing customer orders based on a simple description like "Create a workflow that receives orders, checks inventory, and sends a confirmation email."

LangFlow will incorporate tools that leverage AI and natural language processing (NLP) to automatically generate workflows. These tools will streamline the development process by understanding the user's intent and creating appropriate nodes and workflows based on that input.

19.4. LangFlow in Edge Computing

Edge computing is the practice of processing data closer to where it is generated, such as on IoT devices, rather than sending it to centralized cloud servers. LangFlow is perfectly suited for edge computing, enabling real-time decision-making and processing at the source.

LangFlow can be deployed on edge devices, such as Raspberry Pi, microcontrollers, or other IoT devices, to process data locally and reduce latency. These edge deployments are especially useful for applications like real-time monitoring, smart homes, and autonomous vehicles.

Example: Deploying LangFlow on an Edge Device: LangFlow can be installed and run on an edge device like Raspberry Pi to process sensor data locally without relying on cloud services. This setup enables real-time actions, such as activating alarms or adjusting controls, based on local data analysis.

Benefits:

- **Reduced Latency**: By processing data locally, edge computing reduces the time it takes for devices to respond to inputs.
- **Lower Bandwidth Usage**: Reduces the amount of data sent to the cloud, saving bandwidth and reducing costs.
- **Enhanced Privacy**: Sensitive data can be processed and stored locally, ensuring better privacy.

Challenges:

- **Limited Resources**: Edge devices typically have less processing power and storage than cloud servers, so LangFlow workflows may need to be optimized for these environments.
- **Complexity in Management**: Managing edge devices at scale can be more complex compared to centralized cloud environments.

19.5. Predictions for the Future of LangFlow

LangFlow's adaptability and its integration with the latest technologies make it a powerful tool for the future. As AI, machine learning, and other emerging technologies continue to evolve, LangFlow will be a central platform for developing intelligent workflows.

- **Advanced AI Models**: Future versions of LangFlow will likely include support for even more sophisticated AI models, allowing for enhanced automation and decision-making.
- **Increased Integration Capabilities**: LangFlow will continue to expand its ability to integrate with emerging technologies like blockchain, AR/VR, and edge computing.
- **Improved User Interface**: Enhancements to the LangFlow UI will make it even easier for developers to create, debug, and manage workflows, incorporating more drag-and-drop functionality and real-time collaboration tools.

LangFlow will play a key role in the evolving AI landscape by:

- **Bridging the Gap**: LangFlow helps bridge the gap between AI models and real-world applications, allowing developers to integrate cutting-edge AI technologies seamlessly into their workflows.
- **Enabling Automation**: LangFlow will continue to be a leading platform for automating complex tasks across industries, from customer service to healthcare to finance.

As the AI landscape evolves, LangFlow will remain at the forefront, providing developers with the tools they need to build intelligent, scalable, and efficient workflows.

This chapter has explored some of the exciting trends and innovations that will shape LangFlow in the future. From advancements in AI and machine learning to integration with emerging technologies like blockchain and AR/VR, LangFlow is poised to be a powerful platform for building the next generation of intelligent workflows. As LangFlow continues to evolve, its role in edge computing, automated workflow generation, and the broader AI ecosystem will only grow, making it an essential tool for developers looking to create cutting-edge solutions.

Chapter 20: Appendix and Resources

This final chapter provides a comprehensive collection of resources to help you further your understanding and mastery of LangFlow. Whether you're looking for definitions of technical terms, a guide to LangFlow's command-line interface (CLI), sample code repositories for hands-on practice, or additional reading materials and community support, this chapter serves as a useful reference.

20.1. Glossary of Terms

To ensure that you fully understand the key concepts and terminology used throughout this book and in LangFlow, we've compiled a glossary of common terms. This section defines the most important concepts and explains technical jargon that you may encounter when working with LangFlow.

- **LangFlow**: A framework designed to help developers build, deploy, and manage AI-powered workflows by connecting various AI components (agents, nodes, and services) in a modular way.
- **Node**: A functional unit in a LangFlow workflow that performs a specific task, such as data processing, transformation, or integration with external services.
- **Workflow**: A series of interconnected nodes that process data and execute tasks in a specific sequence to accomplish a business process or AI task.
- **Agent**: A LangFlow component that manages a collection of workflows and coordinates interactions between them.
- **API (Application Programming Interface)**: A set of protocols and tools that allow different software applications to communicate with each other. LangFlow integrates with APIs to extend its capabilities and access external services.
- **Machine Learning Model**: An algorithm or system trained on data to make predictions or decisions without being explicitly programmed. LangFlow can integrate various machine learning models into workflows.

- **Smart Contract**: A self-executing contract with the terms of the agreement directly written into code, typically used on blockchain platforms. LangFlow can automate interactions with smart contracts for use cases like decentralized finance (DeFi).
- **ETL (Extract, Transform, Load)**: A process used in data integration to extract data from different sources, transform it into a suitable format, and load it into a destination (e.g., a database or data warehouse).
- **Latency**: The time delay between sending a request and receiving a response, typically used to measure the speed of data processing or communication in a network.
- **Scalability**: The ability of a system or application to handle an increasing amount of work or to be easily expanded to accommodate growth.
- **CI/CD (Continuous Integration and Continuous Deployment)**: A set of practices in software development that involve automatically integrating code changes and deploying them to production with minimal manual intervention.
- **Containerization**: A lightweight form of virtualization that allows developers to package an application and its dependencies into a single, portable container for consistent deployment across different environments.

20.2. Comprehensive LangFlow CLI Commands Reference

LangFlow's Command-Line Interface (CLI) offers a set of powerful commands that allow developers to interact with the framework directly from the terminal. This section provides a detailed listing of the most commonly used LangFlow CLI commands, along with examples of how to use them.

1. langflow init:

- Initializes a new LangFlow project by creating the necessary files and folder structure.

Example:
bash

langflow init my_project

- This command sets up a new LangFlow project named my_project.
2. **langflow start**:
   - Starts the LangFlow server and begins executing workflows.

Example:
bash

langflow start

- Use this command to start LangFlow and begin processing data through your workflows.
3. **langflow deploy**:
   - Deploys the current LangFlow project to a specified environment (e.g., local server, cloud).

Example:
bash

langflow deploy --environment=production

- This command deploys the current project to the production environment.
4. **langflow status**:

- Checks the status of the LangFlow agent and workflows, including whether they are running or have encountered errors.

Example:
bash

```
langflow status
```

5. langflow logs:
   - Displays the logs of the currently running workflows and agents to help with debugging.

Example:
bash

```
langflow logs --tail
```

- The --tail flag shows the most recent log entries.
6. langflow install:
   - Installs dependencies or plugins for LangFlow.

Example:
bash

```
langflow install langflow-plugin-example
```

- Installs a third-party plugin named langflow-plugin-example.

Starting a Workflow:
bash

```
langflow start workflow_name
```

Deploying a Project to the Cloud:
bash

```
langflow deploy --environment=cloud
```

Checking the Status of a Node:
bash

```
langflow status node_name
```

Viewing the Logs of a Specific Workflow:
bash

```
langflow logs --workflow=workflow_name --tail
```

These CLI commands provide direct control over LangFlow's operation and help streamline development and deployment processes.

20.3. Sample Code Repositories

LangFlow's open-source nature means there are numerous code repositories available that contain example projects and reusable components. These repositories provide valuable resources for learning and building your own LangFlow workflows.

LangFlow's official GitHub repository contains several example projects that demonstrate how to use the framework in different contexts. These include workflows for:

- **Data processing and transformation**
- **AI model integration**
- **API and service integration**
- **Real-time data processing**

You can access these example projects by visiting the LangFlow GitHub Repository.

- LangFlow Main Repository: The official LangFlow repository contains the source code, documentation, and community contributions.
- LangFlow Example Projects: A collection of example projects showcasing different use cases for LangFlow.
- LangFlow Plugins: A repository for LangFlow plugins, where developers can contribute and download extensions for the platform.

These repositories serve as both a learning resource and a starting point for your LangFlow projects.

20.4. Additional Reading and Tutorials

In addition to the resources provided in this book, there are numerous external materials that can help deepen your understanding of LangFlow and related technologies. This section provides recommendations for further reading and learning opportunities.

- **"Deep Learning with Python" by François Chollet**: This book provides a comprehensive introduction to deep learning, with practical examples using Keras and TensorFlow, which can be useful for integrating AI models with LangFlow.

- **"Designing Data-Intensive Applications" by Martin Kleppmann**: A great resource for understanding data systems and architectures, which is highly relevant when building complex workflows in LangFlow.
- **"The Pragmatic Programmer" by Andrew Hunt and David Thomas**: A timeless book that covers best practices and tips for software developers, including clean code principles that are applicable when building LangFlow workflows.
- **Coursera: Deep Learning Specialization**: A series of courses taught by Andrew Ng that covers deep learning fundamentals and advanced topics, helping you integrate AI models with LangFlow.
- **Udemy: The Complete Node.js Developer Course**: A practical course for developers who want to learn how to build back-end services that integrate with LangFlow workflows.
- **edX: Introduction to Blockchain**: A course that covers the fundamentals of blockchain technology, which is useful when integrating blockchain with LangFlow for applications like supply chain management.

These resources will help you expand your knowledge and skills, allowing you to use LangFlow to its fullest potential.

20.5. Community and Support Channels

LangFlow has an active and growing community of developers who contribute to the project, share knowledge, and offer support. Engaging with the community can provide valuable assistance and insights when you're troubleshooting, looking for advice, or sharing your own experiences.

- **LangFlow GitHub Discussions**: The GitHub Discussions section of LangFlow's repository is a great place to ask questions, share ideas, and participate in community-driven conversations.

- **Stack Overflow: LangFlow Tag**: The LangFlow tag on Stack Overflow allows users to ask technical questions and get answers from other developers who are using LangFlow.
- **LangFlow Documentation**: The official LangFlow documentation provides comprehensive information on installation, configuration, and usage of LangFlow.
- **LangFlow Support Email**: For more personalized support, you can reach out to LangFlow's support team via email.

By using these resources, you can connect with the LangFlow community and gain access to a wealth of knowledge and expertise to help you succeed with your LangFlow projects.

This chapter has provided a variety of valuable resources to support your continued learning and development with LangFlow. Whether you're looking for a glossary of terms, a detailed CLI reference, sample code, or additional reading materials, this appendix serves as a comprehensive guide for further exploration. Additionally, the community and support channels offer ongoing assistance to help you overcome challenges and stay up-to-date with LangFlow's latest developments.

Index

An index serves as an essential tool for quickly navigating through a book, helping readers locate specific topics, concepts, and terms with ease. It allows for efficient access to information, especially in technical books like this one on LangFlow. This section will help you find key terms, topics, and examples that are mentioned throughout the book, making it easier to refer to specific sections or concepts. The index is organized alphabetically, with subheadings and page references to guide you through the content.

This index provides a thorough and organized way to locate topics and terms referenced throughout the book. Whether you are looking for technical definitions, usage examples, or practical implementation guides, the index will help you quickly find the information you need to enhance your understanding of LangFlow and build sophisticated workflows. By referring to the page numbers, you can delve into the relevant sections for detailed explanations, examples, and best practices to help you leverage LangFlow to its fullest potential.

www.ingramcontent.com/pod-product-compliance
Lightning Source LLC
LaVergne TN
LVHW081524050326
832903LV00025B/1622